CALLED TO BE ME

Deaconess Margaret Cundiff was born in Somerset but has lived in the north of England since early childhood. Since 1973 she has served on the staff of a busy parish church in North Yorkshire. She is also Broadcasting Officer for the diocese of York, Anglican adviser to Yorkshire Television, and broadcasts regularly on Radio Humberside and Radio Leeds. She is a member of the General Synod of the Church of England. All this she combines successfully with a happy family life, as home-maker to her husband, son and daughter.

Called to be
me

MARGARET CUNDIFF

Illustrations by
Brian Tutt

TRIANGLE

First published 1982
Triangle/SPCK
Holy Trinity Church
Marylebone Road
London NW1 4DU

Second impression 1984
Third impression 1985

British Library Cataloguing in Publication Data

Cundiff, Margaret
  Called to be me.
  1. St. James's Church (*Selby*)   2. Deaconesses
  —England—Selby (North Yorkshire)
  3. Church work
  I. Title
  262'. 14342845   BV4424.C5
  ISBN 0-281-04013-3

Filmset, printed and bound in Great Britain by
Hazell Watson & Viney Limited,
Member of the BPCC Group,
Aylesbury, Bucks

For Peter
Julian and Alison
and my parents
and all who have helped
me to be me

CONTENTS

FOREWORD

You will enjoy reading this book. It is full of reminiscences, painful and hilarious, of an unusually interesting and uncompromising life which, as you will see, had such an unpromising beginning. It will tell you about Margaret Cundiff's vocation to the ministry and all that it has meant to her. But it will also tell you of her vocation to be herself, the self she was born with and the self she became under the influence of Christ. It will also tell you something about the Church in the north of England which she has served with great vigour and devotion. It will tell you . . . but then you must read it for yourself, as I have done with great profit and amusement.

STUART EBOR:

ACKNOWLEDGEMENTS

I would like to express my grateful thanks to all those who have encouraged me to discover God's way for my life, by their wise counsel, loving concern and prayerful support:

the Archbishop of York, Dr Stuart Blanch,
the Bishop of Selby, the Right Revd Morris Maddocks,
and Miss Christian Howard,
who have enabled me to fulfil my ministry as a deaconess
in the diocese of York;

and the clergy and congregation of
St James' Church, Selby, North Yorkshire,
who for twelve years have allowed me to minister with
and amongst them.

My special thanks to my editor, Miss Myrtle Powley, whose idea this book was, and who has given unstintingly of her professional skills and personal friendship; also to Brian Tutt for illustrating my life so delightfully in these pages.

MARGARET CUNDIFF

1

THE SURVIVOR

'She won't live, of course,' said the sister. Nearly three months premature, the tiny scrap of humanity lay helpless as a young bird, panting, ugly, wizened, and weighing all of two-and-three-quarter pounds.

Outside in the night, the wind howled and the rain lashed down. The streets of Minehead seemed deserted. Not even a stray dog was out. The tide came in with winter fierceness, pounding against the sea wall. It was a bleak welcome for the child who had come far too early into the world and from which it seemed she was to depart with equal haste.

'No, she can't possibly survive.' The sister shook her head sadly. 'Still, it's a blessing really. The parents are so young, and the father is out of work. There will be others, when they get on their feet.'

Grannie, when she arrived the next day, agreed. 'It's best if she dies here,' she tried to comfort her daughter. 'It would be awful if we took her home and learned to love her and then lost her. Better now, before we get to know her.'

The mother refused to give in so easily. 'But I already love her,' she sobbed bitterly. 'I can't just let her go. Make her live!' she demanded. 'Make her live!'

Grannie took a long look at the little bag of bones, now an ominous blue colour, but still breathing. This baby was a fighter. She squared her shoulders. 'All right, love,' she promised. 'We'll make her live!'

And she did. With no incubator, no special nursing care, just lots and lots of love, the baby held on to life by a thread, loved into living, growing. They took her home to the house near the church in the village of Dunster, which the young couple shared with her grandparents. For the first few weeks she was wrapped in cotton wool, cleaned with olive oil, fed from a dropper. Her grandfather would hold her in the palm of his hand, marvelling that something so small could be a real person, with an identity and name of her own—Margaret.

And so I spent the first year of my life within the sound of the church clock striking the hours, and the bells which played hymn tunes. I slept so well that I had sometimes to be woken up by being placed by the gramophone. Unaware of the sacrifice of the little family struggling to keep me alive, I thrived on love, passed through the first critical months, and caught up with life.

The year was 1932, and then as now jobs were hard to find. My parents eventually obtained work in Cheshire, in domestic service. The small cottage which went with the job was enough to persuade them to leave the lovely Somerset countryside and travel several hundred miles to what was a foreign and alien environment. The work was hard, the hours long, and it was badly paid; but at least it was work, and a roof over their heads. Later they moved to another job near Congleton, and it was there that I grew from a toddler to a little girl, started school and Sunday school, joined the Brownies and then the youth group. There we spent the war years when, sheltering under the stairs, I slept the nights away as soundly as I had next to the gramophone, oblivious to the drone of aircraft overhead and the distant gunfire over nearby Manchester.

Even as a child, I was conscious of injustice in a world of haves and have-nots. I saw how my parents were treated because they lived in a tied house and were domestic servants. I hated the way my father was called 'Smith' and had to touch his cap and call his employers Sir or Madam.

I hated the way my mother was at the beck and call of people who seemed to delight in ordering her to work when they knew she wanted to be with her family. So I grew up an angry child, determined to change the lot of my parents and the likes of them. Photographs taken at this time show a round, cross-looking little girl with a way of furrowing her brows in a ferocious manner when she did not like the way things were going.

It seemed I was always in a hurry. In a hurry to get into the world, to get on with life, to get life altered. At school I was bright but difficult. I soon became bored with lessons and lost interest easily unless the subject was something that I felt deeply about. There were many battles between teachers and myself. 'Could do better' turned to 'Must do better', and later, 'Will not try'. I was no conformist.

Although a born leader, I was lonely. The sister in the nursing home had been wrong. There were no more children for the young couple. My mother had a miscarriage when I was twelve, and I grew up an only child. My constant companion was a mongrel dog, as determined a character as I was.

Strangely enough the place where I was happiest was at church. Mossley church was nothing much to look at either inside or out, yet to me it was very special. The vicar was a middle-aged man with five daughters of his own. He was no preacher, but he conveyed by what he was the love of God. Himself from a poor family, he knew what it was like to struggle. He rode round the parish on an old bike, and he knew everyone and cared for everyone, regardless of who or what they were. He was my best friend. I shared with him my anger and frustration, my hopes and dreams. He got me out of scrapes, pleaded my case with parents, teachers and employers. Never once did he turn me away, never showed anything but gentleness and understanding. He was always available, always ready to listen.

3

It was a strange friendship, this angry little girl and the gentle priest. Often I would go into church during the week and see him kneeling alone. As I passed by his study window I would see him on his knees, and it was, I believe, due to his prayers that I began bit by bit to understand more of the Christian faith and what it was all about. Sundays for me were special, with the liturgy, the vestments, the candles, the 'other-worldliness'. I remember thinking, 'If I were a boy I perhaps could have become a priest.'

But I wasn't, and I couldn't, and that was that.

Although passionately interested in the Church, I kept it in a special compartment of my life. For the rest of the time I was in the world, and determined to let the world know I was in it. I thought the way to make a better society was through political action, and I became an ardent socialist. Here, I felt, was the answer to the crying needs of the world, of my country and of my own people. Equality of opportunity would ensure a just society, and the problems would disappear. I had yet to learn the hard way that political theory and political practice are poles apart.

My first job after leaving secondary school was in a factory canteen as an apprentice cook. It was hard work, hot and unexciting. I did it with neither enthusiasm nor dislike. But unknown to me the vicar had been to see the managing director to tell him I was wasted in the canteen, and had asked if he could find me something in the office. So without much notice I was moved into the accounts office, there to learn costing, and I hated it! Soon I decided our ways must part, and after a couple of other jobs, settled down as a wages clerk in a small company.

One day the company secretary commented, 'I don't know what you are doing here. Your heart is not in your job. You should go in either for religion or politics.' Religion or politics? It seemed a very strange choice!

It was then that God stepped in. At a Youth for Christ

rally I was converted, literally 'turned round' in my tracks. This kind of religion was something entirely new in my experience. The preacher did not wear robes. The hymns were very strange, with much clapping and chorus singing. It had me confused. Surely this was not what Christianity was all about! I went to the monthly rallies because a friend had invited me, but I vowed each one would be the last, until one Saturday evening, listening to a Baptist minister, the Reverend Alan Redpath, speaking on the need to be 'born again', I realized this was for me.

All my life I'd assumed I was a Christian. After all, I went to church, I'd been baptized, confirmed, through Sunday school, youth club. I 'belonged'. But that night I realized that being a Christian was more than all that; it was knowing Jesus, not just knowing about, or even approving, what Jesus had done. I met him, just as one person meets another, and I knew what he had done he had done for me. 'Jesus died for me'—but more than this, now I wanted to be able to say, 'Jesus lives in me. I belong to him. He is in charge of my life.'

On the bus coming home from Hanley I silently committed myself to Christ. 'Born again' somewhere between Hanley and Biddulph on a Potteries Motor Traction bus!

The first to be told were my parents. 'I've become a Christian,' I announced.

They didn't flicker an eyelid. 'Of course you are,' said my mother. 'You always have been.'

With the impatience of a crusader, my next stop was the vicarage. 'You never preached the gospel, never told me the truth,' I accused the vicar. 'You shouldn't wear vestments, or have candles; the real Christians don't.'

That dear saintly man just stood there and took it. Then he remarked, 'Perhaps you'd be happier going to St Peter's. Their services would be more what you would like.' So to St Peter's I went.

I never really felt part of St Peter's. Oh yes, I joined the choir and became a bellringer, but I knew that my heart was really in Mossley, and still my best friend was the one on whom I had rounded so strongly. He never gave up. My defection did not affect our friendship at all, and when, only a matter of months later, I felt God was calling me to serve him in a full-time capacity, it was he who supported me and pleaded with my parents to allow me to try for selection and college. It was he who prayed for me and with me.

To the surprise of everyone (except the vicar and myself), I was accepted for training as a parish worker. With high hopes and no resources, I set off for St Michael's House, Oxford, to study there for the next two years. With no money, little talent, and certainly no educational qualifications I possessed an optimism founded on the belief that God would provide, and I slept as soundly as I had done by the gramophone and under the stairs during the air raids. Let others worry, not me!

How did I survive? By the grace of God, and the love of my parents, tutors, fellow-students and friends. They may not have understood me, this teenager who went through life like a whirlwind, often leaving a trail of chaos behind her, with her broad northern accent and her lack of 'finesse'. Gaily I pushed aside all obstacles and joined in everything with equal enthusiasm, from the Oxford University Socialist Society to the Christian Union. Whether at wild parties or in prayer meetings, I lived life to the full with little discrimination. So although my escapades were greeted by 'You'll never guess what Margaret has done now', and no doubt urgent pleas to the Lord for my safety, they loved me, protected me and supported me.

Politics or religion? For me, they went together, and at the end of my time at St Michael's I had little clue as to my future. I was offered a place at a college in Wales for further study in social work. I considered teaching. But in the end I found myself a parish worker in a large Midlands parish.

Who says God has no sense of humour?

2

THE FAILURE

Towards the end of our time in college, we were urged to 'seek the place of the Lord's choice'. I wasn't too sure how one would know this place, but was assured that if I prayed, all would be revealed.

As one by one my fellow-students announced that their 'place' had been found, I became increasingly uneasy. My own prayers didn't seem to be working. I decided to draw up a blueprint of my ideal job.

It would have to be in a seaside town. Not that I was given to beach missions or anything of that nature, but I did like the seaside. I did not really mind what the church itself was like, being very open-minded as to variations in liturgy and practice, but I did have a very clear picture of the vicar—tall, with wavy hair and his own teeth, aged around thirty and unmarried. Life in a parish was going to be just great.

One warm afternoon as I was happily day-dreaming in a deck chair on the college lawn, I saw approaching the front door an elderly, white-haired clergyman. He carried a stick, wore glasses, and although I never discovered for sure, I do not think those were his own teeth. He was the vicar of a large Midlands parish, of which the chief claim to fame was a huge rubber factory, and which was certainly situated nowhere near any sea. This man was to become my first vicar, my seaside parish was nearer to Birmingham than Bournemouth, and any paddling I was going to do would be confined to soaking my aching feet in the bath.

So Sister Margaret arrived! There was no welcoming committee, only a Church Army sister on the verge of retirement and a spindly, black-gowned verger to witness my coming to the parish. It was evident that they were not enthusiastic with this new recruit to the parish team. I was twenty-one, inexperienced and very naïve. My heart sank as I looked from the window of my bedroom at the view over the churchyard. The smell of rubber was already clinging to me as it did to everyone and everything in the area. Where would I start? I wondered. I was soon to find out.

The vicar had obviously decided where I would start—at the bottom! Visiting was to be my main task. I was provided with a large notebook, in which I was to enter each visit, what time I arrived, what time I left, and what I accomplished. I had a large quantity of visiting cards: 'Sister Margaret has called and was sorry to find you out.'

Visiting on those huge council estates was an ordeal by fire—and water! That particular spot in the Midlands must have had the highest rainfall in the British Isles. It would accumulate in the wide brim of my hideous green hat, then trickle down the back of my neck. I quite quickly got to recognize the signs of not being wanted and became remarkably adept at slinking up paths, shooting my visiting card through the letter box and marking my book 'Not at home'. Thank goodness there were some merciful souls who did welcome me in, fed and warmed me, and ministered to me far more than I ever did to them. In the main these people were rough, had very little money, and were completely out of touch with 'the Church', but they shared what they had with me, recognizing someone else as out of her depth with the establishment as they were.

Bit by bit I built up confidence. Listening to them, I began to learn what life was all about for these Midlanders. We shared our doubts, our fears, our joys, our sadnesses. On £250 a year, I was one of them.

As the weeks went by I realized that I was just not cut out for the work of a church sister. The problems I was coming up against were beyond my experience. My elderly vicar had no time to help me, being too busy dealing with the multitude of christenings, marriages and burials which such a large parish provided. I felt far more at ease with non-churchgoers than with the faithful and I grew increasingly despondent that the gifts I knew I had were not being used. In desperation one day I asked the vicar why he had taken me on. Fixing me with a cold stare he replied bluntly, 'Because you were cheaper than a curate!' It did my ego no good at all!

Yet there were highlights. The Boys' Bible Class were my delight, and I was theirs. Where else could they find someone mad enough to explore the woods, play cricket and organize bike races? The choirboys found in me an ally, the Brownies a storyteller, and I would spend hours with them making models and pictures. The youngsters had an enthusiasm that I could share, and they responded wholeheartedly. They wanted to know about Jesus, what he did, what he said. Jesus made sense for them; the Church, in the main, did not.

One group that took me to their hearts were those stalwarts of any church, the Mothers' Union. They were a warm-hearted bunch of Christian women. Often ridiculed in their homes, they battled to bring up their children in the Christian way and to live out their faith amongst their neighbours—not easy for most. They were so grateful for the opportunity to meet and ask questions, to learn, to study the Bible, to pray, and I learnt much of real faithfulness from them.

It was through one of the Mothers' Union members that I eventually came to the parting of the ways in the parish, a hard experience at the time but, looking back, the best thing that could have happened to me.

11

It had been an exhausting day at the church fête on the local playing field. As we surveyed the debris at the end we realized just how tired we all were. Mrs Jones put a motherly arm round me. 'You look all in, Sister. Come home with me and have some tea.' I looked at the mess still to be cleared, but the thought of Mrs Jones' tea convinced me, and off I went.

As we munched slices of delicious cake, my hostess said, 'You know what would do you good, Sister? To go to the pictures with our Ernest.' Ernest was my age, a nice young man, who was having a wash and shave before setting off for the cinema.

'I can't do that,' I said. 'It's not allowed.'

'Not allowed? . . . Who would know?' I thought about that one. Who would know? Anyway, it was Saturday, and meant to be my day off.

So Ernest and I went to the pictures. The film was 'Hobson's Choice', starring John Mills. It did do me good. I relaxed, I laughed, and I slept well that night. I woke up to a bright, sunny day, and there was a spring in my step as I went to morning service.

The vicar had obviously not slept well. He looked rather annoyed. He had, he said, 'something to ask in private'.

'Sister,' he said, when we were alone, 'I am profoundly disturbed. I have been informed that last night you went to the pictures . . . I am sure you will be able to correct this information.'

Then and there I saw we were just the wrong combination of people—he, elderly, worn out with responsibility; me, young, carefree and very green. It just wouldn't work. He needed someone older and wiser and with a deal more parochial experience. I needed . . . Well, what did I need? At that moment I didn't know, and frankly I didn't care. I felt free; a door was opening before me. A door marked Exit.

I looked the vicar firmly in the eye, 'Yes, I did go to the pictures. I enjoyed it, it was "Hobson's Choice" and there was no harm done.'

He frowned at me severely. 'Sister, I will see you at the staff meeting at the vicarage on Wednesday.' He left me in no doubt as to what he would tell me then.

The service ended, I politely shook hands with the departing congregation, hung my gown in the vestry and walked out into the sunshine. Down the church path, across the road, into the house. I shut the door, threw my hat, that awful green monstrosity, into the air, and shouted hurrah!

I grinned at myself in the mirror. 'Hobson's choice,' I laughed. 'I'm free!' It was to be many years before I took a church service again.

I kept the hat as a souvenir. I look at it sometimes, and still detect a slight smell of rubber!

3

SECOND CHANCE

It was all a terrible mistake. How had I got myself into such a situation? All I wanted to do at that moment was to turn the car round, go home to my husband and children and forget all about it. But a promise is a promise, and I couldn't go back on it now. The summons to evensong tolled ominously like a funeral bell as I parked the car, took a deep breath and walked up the path.

The churchwarden greeted me cheerfully at the door. 'How nice to see you, Margaret. But I don't know who's taking the service. You've heard the vicar is in hospital?'

'I am,' I said. He looked puzzled. 'I'm taking the service.'

There was a moment of silence, which felt like eternity. 'Oh, yes!' A broad grin spread over his face. We knew each other well, and he was used to my rather peculiar sense of humour.

'Oh, yes,' I said. 'Seriously. And since it's getting late, I'd better go and get ready.'

Convinced but still bewildered, he escorted me to the vestry. The organist was already playing the voluntary. There was no escape! Eyes burned into the back of my head as I walked down the aisle. I announced the first hymn and kept my head down. So far, so good.

'Dearly beloved, the Scripture moveth us in sundry places . . .' The familiar words steadied me, but they sounded odd, coming out of my mouth.

'Let us kneel and confess our sins to Almighty God.' I knelt—and promptly disappeared from view. The vicar was a tall man. I am five feet two. I could not see over the top of the stall. The prayers that evening were delivered from a sideways position.

The lessons were the second hurdle. I must have looked as if I was gazing upwards for inspiration. Actually, I was trying to read from a lectern which was well above my eye level. As the sermon time got nearer, the pulpit grew, and I shrank. I began to realize how Alice in Wonderland had felt. Would I ever make it?

I made it. Clutching on to the sides for support, I opened my mouth. 'In the name of the Father, and of the Son, and of the Holy Spirit . . .' And then I realized; it was 'in the name of' and 'in the power of'. I knew again the assurance of God's presence. He had called me to this job, and he was going to see me through.

The service over, the congregation eyed me curiously. They'd known me a long time, but not in this rôle. 'We didn't know you did this sort of thing.' 'Well, you are a dark horse!'

My secret was out. Parish worker, trained and failed! I had thought it was all behind me, a year out of my life to put down to experience, but not to be repeated under any circumstances. My training had been done over twenty years ago, my one year in parish work had proved a disaster. Why couldn't God have found someone else? I drove home with mixed feelings, and with an odd suspicion that there were more surprises ahead.

Peter looked up from his book as I entered. 'Had a good time, dear? Was it all right?'

'Yes,' I answered automatically. Then, 'Yes. Yes I did have a good time, and it was all right.' And it was going to be all right—so long as I remembered to get the stall and pulpit sorted out for next week. Next week . . . Well, it was a long time until then. A lot could happen in a week.

It was twenty years since I had shaken the dust off my feet from that Midlands parish and moved on to new pastures. After that disastrous experiment, I went into youth work full time, working in downtown Nottingham, the setting used for the film 'Saturday Night and Sunday Morning'. I enjoyed the challenge of working with young people—and older ones, too. The responsibility was good for me, and it was fun to be able to do things my own way.

It was a chance remark by Jill, one of my voluntary helpers, a social science student, that opened the next chapter of my life. 'You ought to go in for personnel management,' she suggested.

Personnel management? The more I thought about it, and read about it, the more it sounded like a good idea—not least the salary and the hours. I applied to a large textile combine in Manchester and was appointed.

From the first day of my new job I knew I had made the right decision. My early experience of the canteen and office work had made me aware of the lives of those who worked in industry. Theological college had taught me to understand the spiritual nature of man, to experience the power of God at work in the Church. The year in parish work had given me insights into the life of the Christian community, and Nottingham had made me well aware of what went on outside church, home or work. I was growing up. Although inexperienced, I enjoyed being a personnel officer and quickly gained confidence. I loved the people, and they, warm-hearted and loving, responded to me. There was plenty of opportunity to be involved. Clubs, medical and health facilities and personal care were all part of the services provided by the company for employees and pensioners.

But I had more than a career to thank my employers for. I met my husband, Peter, who worked for the same company, though in another of its branches, and in 1960 we married. I continued to work for them until shortly before the birth of our son Julian in 1963. In 1966 Alison was born. I enjoyed my rôle as wife and mother, the pram-pushing, the potty training and the infant school. Life was comfortable and very predictable.

Then came the bombshell. Peter was to be transferred to Yorkshire—across the Pennines! Much as I hated the idea of moving, we realized the change would be for the good of his career and of our family. So reluctantly we moved over the hills into what seemed then to be a bleak and forbidding territory.

The first thing we did was to join a church. Not our local church, but one in the market town five miles from our village. The congregation was warm and welcoming and made us feel at home at once. But from the start we decided not to become too involved. We had our own life, centred on our family. Church was an extra—until again God stepped in!

It happened at a very ordinary Sunday morning service. I was beginning to lose interest in the sermon, which seemed to go on and on. I found myself wondering how the Sunday joint was doing, where we should go with the children in the afternoon . . . until suddenly a voice behind me said, quite distinctly, 'Be filled with the Spirit.'

Startled and embarrassed, I looked round to see who was talking aloud in church. Odd . . . nobody else seemed aware of anything unusual. I tried to concentrate on the service. The voice came again, even more insistent: 'Be filled with the Spirit.' By now, I was feeling distinctly uneasy. Apparently no one else could hear the voice. I took a few deep breaths and told myself firmly, 'You do not hear voices. You are not that sort of person.' The voice seemingly did not get the message. It became even more insistent.

The service was Holy Communion. I made my way forward and knelt at the rail, hoping to have left the voice behind, but it was no good. Again I heard, 'Be filled with the Spirit.'

I gave in. 'Lord,' I prayed, 'I don't understand this at all, but whatever it is, Yes.' Immediately I knew a great peace and joy with an astonishing sense of freedom. I made my bargain there and then. 'All right, Lord, if this is what you want, but I'm keeping quiet about it.'

And keep quiet I did, until a few weeks later when the vicar approached me hesitantly. 'Margaret, may I ask you something? Has . . . has anything happened to you recently?' Embarrassed, I mumbled something and finally blurted out the truth.

He smiled at me. 'You may not have told anyone, but you have certainly changed. You are a different person.'

'But why me?' I asked.

'I don't know,' he told me, 'but God does.'

At the time I hadn't a clue what those words 'Be filled with the Spirit' had meant. I'd heard of those who claimed they had received 'the Baptism of the Spirit'. I knew there were people who were called 'charismatics', and I'd talked to my vicar about this, but felt that it was not for me; and I'd certainly never talked to anyone who claimed to have heard a voice. My initial reaction to the voice had been surprise, then fear, then acceptance. I didn't understand, but I was sure that it was from God and it was right, and that I had to make the decision there and then.

From then on I knew an assurance, a certainty in the power and love of God that I'd never known before; and although there have been many spiritual ups and downs since then, I know that that day a power was released into my life which has never left me.

During the next year we as a family became more involved in the fellowship of the church and also with the new vicar and his wife in the country parish where we lived. We discovered that George's sister and I had been to the same college, and with this link we became good friends. Then one evening came a telephone call to tell us George had had a severe heart attack and was in hospital. We did what we could to help his wife, Peggy, and I remember praying angrily, 'Why, Lord? You have a good man in this place, work going on, and you let this happen. It's not fair. There's no one to do anything here now.'

No one? As I prayed, I realized that there was someone who could do something—me. 'But, Lord, you know I'm no good. I made a mess of it last time.'

It was no use arguing! The next morning I went to see my own vicar. His wife opened the door. 'Oh good, Margaret, I'm glad you've come. We feel you ought to do something about Drax.'

Coincidence? Confirmation? We went to see George in hospital and told him what had happened. 'That's lovely,' he said.

We discussed what needed to be done. Obviously I couldn't take on all of a vicar's duties, but there were many things a lay person could do—visiting, counselling, conducting study groups, taking services of Morning and Evening Prayer (though not, of course, Communion services), even preaching.

Within hours the arrangements had been made with the Bishop for me to look after the parish while George was ill. I felt rather apprehensive, but of course it would only be for a few weeks. I could manage that.

4

LICENSED WOMAN

'We shall have to get you licensed,' the diocesan Secretary for Lay Ministry said firmly. Licensed? I thought. It sounds like what they do to pubs and dogs!

George had by now returned to his parish, but meanwhile my own vicar had left, and I found myself doing a similar job at St James' during the interregnum; it looked as if my temporary status was rapidly becoming permanent. It hadn't even occurred to me that I needed any special authority for this; but Church of England rules must be satisfied, and the machinery was set in motion at once to put matters right.

'I'll get in touch with the Bishop,' the Secretary told me with her customary efficiency. 'He will be able to arrange it.'

Events then rather overtook me—in fact, two events.

We had decided to take a family holiday in South Africa during the summer, which meant among other things various injections. These we arranged to have in May, so that any ill effects, which our doctor assured us were most unlikely, would have subsided by the time we had to travel. 'Only one in a million has any reaction to a smallpox jab,' he remarked airily as he stuck in the needle.

Within days my arms and legs had swollen up, I could hardly walk, and I was covered in angry, weeping sores. Peter and the children were fine. A born coward, I didn't want to make a fuss, but eventually, just a couple of days before my licensing, I gave in and went to the doctor. When he saw the state I was in, he ordered me to bed immediately.

'But I'm going to be licensed on Thursday,' I pleaded.

'Well, you won't be able to go.'

'But I must.'

The doctor looked severe. 'All right, you can get up to go to the service, but that is all.'

I had another thought. 'I'll need my hair doing, can I have an hour up for that?'

He did not look pleased, but relented. 'All right. But if you get any worse, it's hospital for you.'

It had been arranged that my licensing as a Parish Worker should take place during the deanery Eucharist in the Abbey on Ascension Day: it killed two birds with one stone and added an extra incentive for people to come, to see this woman who was to be licensed. The local press had been most intrigued, and headlines proclaimed 'WOMAN TO DO A CURATE'S JOB—FIRST TIME IN 900 YEARS'. Actually, as I was the first woman to be licensed in the Abbey, and the Abbey was 900 years old, it made sense.

We all assembled in the vestry—choir, clergy, deaconesses, other 'licensed women', and, of course, the Bishop. He also was new, and had not licensed a woman before. I was beginning to feel rather nervous. I just hoped that they all knew what they were doing—and anyway, *what* were they doing? By now I was having doubts about the whole thing. I felt rather resentfully that I had been taken over. After all, I was only filling in for a short while for a church that had no one to look after it. It was just for the time being and hardly merited all this performance. However, if this was what they wanted, then so be it.

We lined up for the procession, the choir moved forward, and the hymn began. As I followed on obediently, the Bishop poked me in the ribs.

'Assist me with the chalice,' he said.

'All right,' I agreed, wondering how on earth I was going to cope. What was I supposed to do with the chalice? I had never been allowed to handle one in my early days. Obviously, times had changed, but unfortunately I'd missed out on instruction in this important matter.

I felt another prod. The person walking immediately behind me whispered, 'Ever done it before?'

'No.'

'Well, it's a bit late to tell you what to do, but just remember this: *liquid swings*!'

I have had a great deal of advice in my life, much of it quite useless. This was one of the most valuable tips I have ever received. True indeed, liquid swings—especially in a large, full chalice! Thankfully I remembered my lesson as I assisted the Bishop later in the service.

The moment came for the licensing. I knelt before the Bishop (with difficulty). My smallpox jab was playing me up, the pills I'd taken were making me rather light-headed. I tried to concentrate on what was being said over the top of my head:

'Donald, by Divine Providence, Lord Archbishop of York, to our beloved and approved in Christ, Margaret Joan Cundiff, greeting . . . and so we commend you to Almighty God, humbly praying, in the name of our Lord Jesus Christ, that his blessing may rest upon you and your work.'

The Bishop laid his hands upon my head and prayed for me: 'May the Lord give you wisdom, courage, strength and love to do his will'; and I knew with blinding certainty that this was no temporary measure. I was being licensed, not for 'as long as I felt like it'. This was for life. I had burned my boats.

I stood with the Bishop in the sanctuary of the ancient abbey church, the late evening sun streaming through the windows. The people began to move towards us to take Communion, among them my parents and husband, parishioners and friends. My former vicar, who had returned for the service, knelt down, then looked up at me, shut his eyes

and held out his hands. I often wonder what he prayed then. I rather think it was, 'Oh Lord, don't let her drop it!' I didn't.

That night I knew that I had come home. A lot of seemingly unrelated strands in my life were woven into a whole. I felt excited, yet apprehensive. What was God doing with me? Would I be able to cope? What if I made a mess of it, like last time? So many ifs and buts—and then there came like a trumpet call the words spoken at my confirmation nearly thirty years before, when as a young teenager I had knelt before another bishop, who gave me the words of St Paul: 'I can do all things through Christ, who strengthens me.' No ifs or buts, only 'I can . . . through Christ'.

I came out into the soft evening air, feeling like a teenager again, in joyful anticipation of all that lay before me—and something else: the pain in my arms and legs had gone, the angry sores were cool. Almost overnight I was completely well again, with no more ill effects. Was it coincidence? Was it the medicine taking effect? Or was it . . .?

5

IN AND OUT OF THE CHANCEL

'. . . And do you wear anything to take the service in?' inquired the organist nervously, as he hovered in the vestry doorway, a list of hymns in his hand. I was the visiting preacher, standing in for a vicar who was on holiday, and although the organist had been informed that 'someone' was going to take the service, he obviously had not expected someone like me.

I resisted with difficulty the temptation to say, 'No I do it stark naked!' It's a question I am frequently asked, and I sometimes wonder whether people consider the 'gear' more important than the service itself. Now I am a deaconess it's somewhat easier, as a dark blue cassock, academic hood and deaconess cross are somehow considered 'proper'. As a Licensed Woman Worker I used to wear a maroon gown with what my children called 'Mum's dingly-dangly'—a large inset cross on a white and gold background on a maroon ribbon, sometimes unkindly described as looking like 'first prize at Smithfield'. Clad in such a garment, and with such a title, people could be forgiven for being confused as to my proper function. I've had to put up with remarks ranging from, 'Can't you get anyone else to join you in the choir?' to 'Do you verge?'

Confusion I forgive, rudeness I don't. At an induction in a neighbouring church, we were preparing to move out of the vestry when a pompous-looking little clergyman glared at me and asked, 'And what are *you*?' Leaning forward seductively, I threw out my forty-inch chest and murmured

26

in his ear, 'I'm a Licensed Woman!' I cherish the memory of the look of horror on his face, as he fled in a cloud of dust.

'Really, Margaret,' reproved the Rural Dean, who had overheard this exchange.

I tried to look innocent. 'But that is what I am, it says so on my licence.' And so it does.

In fact, the Church of England seems unable to decide just what such a person should be called, and there are a variety of titles—church worker, woman worker, parish worker, church sister, and no doubt many others. A friend of mine, who was known simply as 'the church worker', was telling a male acquaintance of the trouble she was having with her knees. 'I suppose it's due to all the kneeling I do in church,' she concluded. He looked most concerned. 'Ee, that's not right, love, they ought to get you a hoover.'

A woman preacher, whatever she is called, is still something of a novelty in the Church of England. I vividly remember arriving at a country church to preach and being confronted at the door by a large farmer, who eyed me up and down like an expert appraising livestock.

'Is it you, then?' he asked incredulously.

I told him yes, I was the visiting preacher.

A silence, then: 'Are you married?'

I wondered what bearing this had on my preaching, but admitted to that status.

Again a silence, as he looked very thoughtful. Then he said, 'I feel right sorry for your husband. It must be rotten married to a woman preacher!'

I have to admit this welcome cramped my style a little, but all must have been well, for afterwards he shook me by the hand and said, 'I didn't know what to think about woman parsons before you came, but I quite fancy one now!'

My family have always taken a great interest in my work. I

owe a lot to their encouragement and loving support, even on those occasions when I have proved rather an embarrassment.

Not long after I was licensed, a retired bishop came to St James' to celebrate Holy Communion, and to preach. I was to take the first part of the service and assist in the administration. Though it was the first time I had done it, apart from assisting on the night of my licensing, I was reasonably confident.

Not so my son.

'Are you sure it will be all right, Mum?' he asked as we set out for church. I felt his anxiety was not so much on my account, as for the embarrassment he would feel if his mum made a mess of it.

'There's nothing to worry about,' I assured him confidently. 'I only have to follow the book.'

The bishop must have mistaken me for a seasoned campaigner. He cheerfully rattled off instructions: what part of the service I would take, what he needed, where he would stand. We emerged from the vestry, I formally welcomed the bishop and took a deep breath and launched into the service.

It flowed like a dream. Everything happened in the right place, the atmosphere was relaxed, the congregation responded well. 'Nothing to worry about,' I congratulated myself. 'You can't go wrong so long as you follow the book.'

I followed it . . . until a need to blow my nose caused me to pause for a few seconds.

The bishop chose that moment to announce a hymn, flashing me a friendly smile as he did so. I frowned at him, the congregation launched into 'Love divine, all loves excelling' and, still smiling, he went up the steps into the pulpit.

It was a first-class sermon, and the rest of the service went without a hitch. After the final blessing, we walked together to the door to shake hands with the congregation as they departed.

After a while I left him to go back to the vestry, where he joined me a few minutes later. He was chuckling away.

'I've just been talking to your son,' he said. 'This young boy came up to me and said, "Excuse me, was my mum any good?" I assured him you were.'

I felt pleased and relieved. No mistakes after all. I'd been right, you only had to follow the book.

He smiled again. 'There was just one thing, my dear. You did very well, but there was just one small thing—you bypassed my sermon. "Not to worry," I thought to myself, "When she stops for breath, I'll announce a hymn." '

We looked at each other and both burst out laughing.

'I suppose I'd better come clean,' I said, and confessed my inexperience.

He put a fatherly arm across my shoulders. 'God bless you, my dear; always have courage and don't be afraid to make mistakes. Just go on in faith.'

'Thank you for everything,' I said as I saw him to his car.

'Thank *you*,' he replied.

I went back into the church, stopped and looked at the pulpit.

'Make a note,' I told myself. 'When we have a visiting preacher, make sure you allow him to preach!'

Of all the times in the year for us in the ministry, the most perilous is Harvest Festival, known in the trade as 'Holy Marrowtide'. For sufferers from hay fever the tastefully decorated pulpit can be a disaster area, and even getting into the pulpit through all the lavish foliage is like hacking your way through a jungle.

The highlight of the Harvest Festival (apart of course from the anthem and the harvest supper) is the 'visiting preacher'. For months beforehand, names and addresses are exchanged, with notes on form—'has plenty of funny stories', 'keeps it short' or 'at least you can hear what he says, even if you don't agree with it'.

Since my first unfortunate experience of a man-sized pulpit, I have realized that it is necessary to carry out a survey of a church before actually taking the service, and Peter and I have spent some very pleasant Saturday afternoons looking around churches I am to preach in, testing them for fit. The problem is that members of the church are usually decorating at that time, and I have had some very funny looks as I have tried out the pulpit, lectern and stall. One dear lady looked at me most suspiciously when I explained the reason; when I saw her in the front row the following morning I was tempted to say, 'I told you so.'

Quite my worst experience happened in a delightful village church, beautifully decorated. I arrived for the morning service, to be greeted by a lady brandishing a duster. 'Just getting rid of a few wasps,' she explained brightly. 'They come in for the fruit, you see.'

As I knelt to pray I felt something climbing up my leg inside my cassock. Cautiously I 'swung a leg'. The tickling stopped, and I hoped it had gone away. As the service progressed, I knew it had not. Just before the *Jubilate Deo* it stung me behind the knee. 'O be joyful in the Lord' was more of an 'Oooooh'!

I then spent much of the rest of the service trying to remember whether it was bees or wasps that only sting once. In the hymn before the sermon I leaned back in the pulpit to regain my composure. As I stood up to preach, all I could manage was a strangled squawk. My hood had become entangled in a piece of ancient medieval wood-carving. I dared not pull, for the carving was of great value. I eased myself out of that situation with great difficulty.

Preaching to strange congregations has many perils.

We have also to remember that even our most innocent actions can be misconstrued.

I was invited one Sunday to a lovely old country church in a farming area. The vicar had asked me to take a service for him while he was away, so that his congregation could have the opportunity of seeing a woman in action. It was an evangelical parish, and I had been duly warned, 'They don't turn for the creed, or bow, just do it straight.' Fine, I thought, I'm happy to fit in with what they do.

My arrival occasioned great excitement. The entire choir crowded into the vestry to watch me put on my robes, eager to observe my every move. We moved out to the back of the church, formed a procession and began to walk up the aisle to the strains of the opening hymn. Suddenly I realized that my 'dingly-dangly' had come undone and had slipped inside my bra. I quickly put my books on the floor, retrieved my badge of office and fastened it, and in seconds had straightened up behind the choir. All went well, I was received very kindly, and the congregation were obviously satisfied—or so at least I thought.

Some time later I met the vicar in the street. He thanked me for coming, then coughed rather nervously. 'There's just one thing I'd like to ask you about, Margaret,' he said. 'When I inquired how you had got on, the warden said, "She was very good. The only thing we didn't care for was that she was a bit High Church." Whatever did you get up to?'

I thought hard, but couldn't think of anything that would have given them that impression.

The vicar went on; 'I believe it was something that happened at the beginning of the service . . .'

The penny dropped! My 'High Church practice' had been when I had gone down on one knee to fish my badge out of my bra. Which all goes to show that congregations don't miss a trick!

This matter of robes and ceremonies has its reverse aspect.

There was to be a missionary speaker at Evensong in our own church. I arrived to find the warden chatting to a middle-aged man. 'Here's the preacher,' he said. 'You can look after him now.'

I invited our visitor into the vestry. He eyed me curiously and, I thought, with some embarrassment as I put on my robes. I suddenly realized that he had not been carrying the usual small suitcase which is part of the paraphernalia of all visiting Anglican preachers.

'Have you brought your robes?' I asked.

He smiled and shook his head. 'I'm afraid I don't have any.'

Oh well, I thought, he can borrow the Reader's, and I offered them.

He coughed. 'Er—actually, I'm not Church of England.'

'Methodist?' I inquired cheerfully. We are an ecumenically minded church.

He shook his head.

'Baptist?'

'You'll never believe it,' he said. 'I'm Brethren.'

'We've got a problem,' I said. 'You don't allow women to speak in church, but you don't know the Anglican service.'

'That's all right,' he assured me. 'I'm more than happy for you to lead.' He explained that his society was an interdenominational one, and although most of the Secretaries were Anglican, some, like himself, were not.

So, all went smartly—until the end of the service. I had forgotten to explain to him that it is our custom for the clergy to walk to the back of the church during the last hymn. Although I announced a 'recessional hymn', he would not know the drill. I walked over to him.

'Would you like to walk down the aisle with me?' I whispered in his ear.

'It would be my pleasure,' he replied.

As we walked down side by side I wondered what his Brethren Assembly would have said. I hope they would have been happy. After all, what did it matter really? What was important was that two Christians had helped each other to proclaim the love of God. It is no use talking about mission, and about our oneness in Christ, if we are not prepared to put aside our preconceived ideas and depart from our set ways. Here we were, in the formal setting of Anglican Evensong, psalms and chants and all, he in a plain lounge suit, me, a woman, dressed up in odd attire, yet there had been no unease as we knelt together, fellow-workers, for Christ, in Christ.

And that, after all, is what it is all about.

6

. . . TO PREACH THE WORD

'It won't do, you know, Margaret.' The message was clear, as if the words had been actually spoken.

'You could have told me earlier, Lord,' I remonstrated. But of course, he had tried to tell me. It was just that I hadn't listened. I knew very well that it wouldn't do.

'It' was the sermon which I was about to preach. I'd had a warning feeling all week about that sermon. On paper it looked all right, but it was lacking something. 'Still,' I thought, 'it will be all right on the night.' But now it was the night, it was the hymn before the sermon, and on my knees I knew for sure, dead sure, that it was no good.

'Ah, well, here goes.' I rose from my knees, walked into the pulpit and preached.

I might as well have saved my breath. The congregation had that glazed look which spells death to any sermon. I could feel the words coming back and hitting me with a dull thump around the ears. Frantically I tried to arouse my slumbering audience, but it was no use. They only came to life as I said Amen.

'What happened to you tonight?' the vicar asked when we were in the vestry.

'It was a shocker, wasn't it,' I admitted shamefacedly.

He agreed! 'But it wasn't just the sermon, it was you. Something happened between the time you knelt down to pray and when you got up. You didn't look at me, you didn't smile and you seemed to drag yourself into the pulpit.'

Peter said much the same thing as we drove home. 'Not one of your better efforts tonight, was it? What went wrong?'

What had happened was that I had decided that the congregation needed to be told certain things, and had forgotten that what matters in preaching is not what we ourselves want to say, but the truth that God wants to convey through us. However polished my words, they never had any life because I wasn't really convinced myself that they were the right words—and therein lies the difference.

Fortunately, it's not very often like that, for, as my vicar is always telling me, 'The Lord is gracious!'

On the other hand, there are those glorious occasions when everything does go right, when one has the joyful experience of being lifted completely out of one's thoughts into the state of being a listener. I have known times when it has been as though I were standing beside someone else, hearing a message from God that was exactly right for me. To be bowled over by one's own sermon! Yet as preachers, can we ever claim that it is 'our sermon'? Perhaps it is only when the sermon speaks to us that it is truly God's word, that it has indeed the breath of life.

One Lent I was invited to preach in a West Yorkshire church. It was an evening service, in midweek. I asked the vicar how long the service was supposed to last.

'Oh, it is contained within the hour,' he told me. 'We have shortened Evensong and sermon.'

It was a lovely church, and I felt an atmosphere of warm anticipation. The service was worshipful, relaxing, and by the time I went into the pulpit I felt totally at ease. As I preached, I became even more relaxed. I could sense the response of the congregation to what I was saying, feel their participation and their eagerness. When I was well into my stride I flung out my arm (I tend to throw my arms about quite a lot when I preach) and noticed my watch. To my horror I realized I had been preaching for an hour. I rounded my sermon off as quickly as I could without losing the points.

As I stood at the church door shaking hands afterwards I half expected some fierce remarks about the length. None came. Maybe nobody had noticed the time, I thought hopefully.

Then I saw the old lady. Very old and very bent, she was walking towards me with difficulty.

'Oh dear,' I thought, 'it's probably long past her bedtime, and sitting for so long can't have done her any good. I must apologize.'

She came up and grasped my hand and smiled. 'Thank you ever so much, love, it was a real help to me.'

'Kind of you to say so,' I answered, 'but I'm sorry I went on for so long. I do apologize.'

The old hand tightened on mine. 'Ee, don't you worry about that, love, there's all tomorrow not touched yet.'

I sometimes remind my own congregation of that remark when they complain about the length of my sermons.

But they do get their own back!

One Christmas morning at the family service I was preaching about the gifts the kings brought.

'You see,' I said, 'when we give gifts, we try to make them appropriate.' And I went on to describe suitable presents for various kinds of people—footballs for footballers, torches for people who have to go out in the dark, perfume for girls who like going to discos, etc. Then I produced my own Christmas gift from my husband—a stopwatch.

'In my work this is a very appropriate gift,' I said, meaning my work in broadcasting, when I have to time programmes.

37

From somewhere in the front pews came a swift retort: 'A gift from a very wise man, I presume.'

Point taken!

Preaching is a strange experience, for no two occasions are ever quite the same. You can never be sure what will happen, even when you have carefully prepared beforehand.

There is nothing to equal that special excitement when it turns out that just one sentence, or one phrase, has been to a person the word from God that makes all the difference to his life. It is on these occasions that we experience the enormous privilege of knowing that we are a channel through which God can speak.

Some years ago I was invited to preach in our famous and historic Abbey. Rather overawed by the honour, I prepared my sermon extra carefully, tailoring it, I felt, for that particular congregation. I delivered it carefully, and had reached the end when I felt strongly moved to go on and make a special appeal, a thing I seldom do.

'If there is anyone here who has reached the end of his tether, who has lost all hope, then remember this,' I urged. 'You may be feeling that no one cares, no one understands, no one can help. Please, if you feel like this, just shout "Help!" to the Lord. He will hear, and I promise he will help you. He will transform your situation, not in the future, but right *now*!'

No one in the congregation looked remotely in need of that advice, and I had no idea why I felt I had to say it. All I knew was that the words demanded to be said.

When the service was over, I was approached by a well-dressed, middle-aged man who asked to speak to me.

'My life is in ruins,' he told me. 'I am on my way from London to Edinburgh, and as I was driving along I thought to myself, "There is absolutely no point in life, no hope. Why do I go on?" When I got this far I decided I must stop for a while and rest, and try to make some sense out of the muddle. I saw the church and came in and sat right at the back. The service was almost finished, and someone was speaking. At first I couldn't hear what the voice was saying, then I heard it say that if I was in trouble, I should just shout "Help" to the Lord. So I shouted "Help", and God did hear me. He has answered, and I now know what I have to do. I know there is hope. The clouds have lifted. I am a different man.'

We talked for a while, and it was quite evident that the Lord had dealt with his situation. I walked with him to his car, and he got in, waved to me and drove off. As he turned the corner he gave a cheerful toot on his horn, and to me it sounded like a shout of victory.

What did Paul write to the Corinthians? It pleased God, through the folly of what we preach, to save those who believe.

7

THE CHURCH IS PEOPLE

One of the pleasures of being 'the visiting preacher' so
often is that there is a chance to experience all shades of
churchmanship, and all possible variations of liturgy. I
admit to rather enjoying ceremonial at times, and it seems
a pity that we cannot arrive at a happy medium between
the rather too matey-with-God attitude of some evangelical
churches and the elaborate ritual of Anglo-catholicism—
and, of course, the hand-waving charismatics. There is
room for all in the Church of England, and it is just a
pity we can't accept each other for what we are, and
combine the best of all worlds.

But everyone is entitled to his pet dislike, and mine is the
jolly-jolly attitude which some people exhibit towards the
exchange of the 'peace'. Though by nature an extrovert,
being swept into a stranger's arms in the middle of a service
is not my idea of either worship or fun.

This feeling is shared by Michael, our church treasurer,
so we usually sit together when we go to a deanery or
diocesan service and solemnly shake hands at the appropriate
moment.

However, we came unstuck one day. The celebrant was
very keen that we should all share the peace with enthusiasm
and as Michael and I shook hands he came between us and
planted a smacking kiss on my cheek. Michael stared in
horror and backed away, knocking over several chairs in his
panic. 'If he'd have come near me, I'd have said, geroff!' he
muttered as he picked up the scattered furniture.

Poor Michael, it really put him off! We need to be sensitive to one another, and to realize that it takes all sorts to make a world; that it doesn't mean a person is any less loving or committed if he or she doesn't take kindly to being hugged and kissed.

Yet there are times when a loving physical gesture can mean so much.

For years, Mrs Walker, a quiet little widow, had attended St James's on Sunday mornings. She declined all invitations to join in other activities, choosing to sit by herself week after week.

One Sunday, as I was shaking hands at the door, I put my arm round her and gave her a hug. I completely forgot about the incident until the following Sunday when she came up to me and shyly said, 'I want to thank you for what you did for me last week.'

'What was that?' I thought hard. 'I wasn't preaching last Sunday.'

She smiled. 'You put your arm round me, and hugged me. It's years since anyone did that.'

From then on, she seemed to come out of her shell, join in parish activities and become a real character. Somehow a hug had released her.

This taught me an important lesson. I now look at the congregation Sunday by Sunday and realize how many of them are alone. How long since someone put an arm round them, gave them a kiss, or even shook their hand? Sometimes words are useless; a hand or an arm is more eloquent. We all need to learn that we are body as well as mind and soul. Our bodies, too, can express our sympathy, our love, our care.

So there is room for both the Michaels and the Mrs Walkers. It's just a matter of knowing how to respond in the right way to individuals, respecting them for what they are.

Old Mr Thomas, a long-standing member of the congregation, is a particular favourite of mine, and I enjoy visiting him in his home when infirmity prevents him from coming often to church. He is one of the 'old brigade', forever talking nostalgically of the days 'when parsons were parsons, and folk knew what to expect when they went to church, proper psalms and hymns and proper Prayer Book, none of these new-fangled services'. He has been an Anglican all his life, and delights in telling me of the time when he sang in a cathedral choir; he is, in fact, a very talented musician.

We get on together very well, but for one thing, which he always makes a point of mentioning. 'I like you very much, Mrs Cundiff, you are a good woman, but I don't agree with women in the sanctuary. That's for men and for angels!' Yet he never refuses to accept the chalice from my hands, and I admire him for the fact that his concern for me as a person outweighs his own strong feelings on the subject. However, he can't refrain from giving me a reproachful look whenever I administer the chalice. Often, as I take part in the communion service, I see him nudge the person next to him and pass a Bible open at 1 Corinthians 14, the passage about women keeping silence in church.

I asked him one day why he felt so strongly on the subject.

'It's like this,' he said. 'There were no women at the Last Supper; you can't get away from that. And,' he added with a note of triumph in his voice, 'I've got a photograph to prove it!'

He took me into his 'front room' and there on the wall was a large picture of the Last Supper. I had to admit that it did look rather like a photograph.

'Mr Thomas,' I said, 'if that's a photograph of the Last Supper, hang on to it. It's worth a fortune!'

I think he knew I was teasing him, but if he did, he didn't show it.

Perhaps because I am a woman, or maybe because I was a member of St James' before I was ever licensed, I get the feeling that many of our church members see me as occupying a sort of half-way status between one of the congregation and a 'proper minister'. I come in for a lot of ribbing from those who know me well, and I enjoy this, though it can be disconcerting. Like the time I left a page of my sermon notes in the vestry.

I always prepare my sermons very carefully, typing them out word for word, on the theory that 'if my mind goes blank, I can always read it'. It hasn't happened yet, but it could! Although I take my script into the pulpit, I hardly need to refer to it, apart from headings.

On this particular evening I had put it down on a desk in the vestry, and picked it up just before the service. During the first hymn, Michael, our treasurer, handed me a sheet of paper. 'You may need this,' he whispered.

Hastily I put it in its place with the other sheets and forgot about it until, halfway through my sermon, I saw written across the page, 'Pause for applause'. I caught his eye. There was a distinct pause, but fortunately he did not applaud!

On another occasion, the Bishop had come to conduct a confirmation service. In the vestry beforehand, he asked me, 'Would you be my chaplain?'

'Thank you very much, yes,' said I.

As soon as I got the chance I whispered frantically to James, my vicar, 'What do I do?'

'I don't know. I've never been one.'

Not very helpful! I decided honesty was the best policy. 'Excuse me, Bishop, what do I do?'

He looked puzzled that I should have to ask. 'It's quite simple, just do what I do.'

He couldn't mean that literally, I decided. I would have to play this one by ear.

As the service progressed, I discovered that my job was chiefly to hold his books and pass them to him at the right time. Just before the act of confirmation he handed me his pastoral staff and I stood obediently by his side while he laid his hands on the candidates.

Suddenly I was aware of Michael standing in the congregation with a beatific smile on his face. I wondered what had caught his attention. Everything seemed all right to me.

Afterwards the Bishop thanked me for carrying out my duties so well, and I began to feel quite pleased with myself. After all, it was not every day I was a bishop's chaplain! Then Michael's wife came up to me, convulsed with laughter.

'Oh, Margaret, it was awful!'

I felt rather taken aback. 'Awful? I thought I did it rather well.'

'Oh, no. It wasn't your fault, it was Michael's. In the middle of the confirmation he nudged me and said, "Look at Little Bo Peep!"'

I had to admit that maybe, standing there, I had looked just a tiny bit like that shepherdess.

The next time the Bishop visited us, Michael said to me before the service, 'I hope you are not going to do your Bo Peep act again.'

I put on my best ecclesiastical manner. 'If I'm asked to, I will.' And I was, and I did!

As we solemnly walked up the aisle, I caught the words that Michael was singing to the tune of the hymn as we passed him:

> Little Bo Peep has lost her sheep
> And doant know where to find them . . .

His face was absolutely deadpan!

I still enjoy the role of bishop's chaplain, but I always have to be on the alert for I never know how Michael will

react—I think we have come to an acceptance of each other's thoughts on the subject! I have never been annoyed by his teasing. On the contrary, I take it as a compliment. It shows he recognizes that I, too, have a sense of humour.

Having a giggle is one thing. Actually showing emotion in a service is something else. Typically Anglican, our congregation prefers to ignore any signs of enthusiasm in worship.

'I'm going to wake them up this morning,' said James, as we prepared to process into church. 'Let's put a bit of life into the service. They all look so solemn, you'd never think it was Easter Day.'

As we reached our stalls, before announcing the first hymn, he turned to face the congregation.

'Hallelujah! Christ is risen!' The joyful acclamation rang through the church.

The deathly silence which ensued was broken only by my solo response: 'He is risen indeed!'

As he moved to the pulpit for the sermon, James leaned across to me. 'I'll have another go.'

'Hallelujah! Christ is risen!' he shouted from the pulpit.

A look of blank astonishment appeared on the congregation's faces.

'I'm not going to be beaten,' James muttered during the last hymn, 'I'll have one more go.'

So he gave the blessing, and then with all the power he could muster he roared, 'Hallelujah! Christ is risen!'

Absolutely no response. His eyes met mine. 'Nothing doing,' they clearly said.

As I stood by the door after the service, an elderly member of the congregation came up to me, looking anxious. 'What were Vicar getting so excited about this morning?'

I explained that as it was Easter Day, he had felt it would be good to rejoice in this way.

'Oh, is that all.' A look of relief came into her face. 'I thought mebbe summat important had happened!'

However, I have long since discovered that the absence of vocal affirmation does not mean a lack of response. I have been very much moved when folk from our congregation have approached me, often very shyly, and shared with me their spiritual experience, their down-to-earth faith.

One such person was Fred. Week by week he and his wife had come to church, but had said very little. Then, just before they moved away from the district, Fred said to me, 'I shall miss the church here. Do you know what I'd like to do? I'd love to read a lesson one Sunday before we leave. Do you think I could?'

I readily agreed. We were without a vicar at the time, so I was glad in any case to have some help.

'I'll need a rehearsal, you know,' he said, and so a couple of days before the service we met in church for a practice and he read beautifully. Afterwards I could see he was wanting to say something, so I waited quietly for him to speak.

'I want to tell you something. Some time ago you preached on healing, and you talked about the "laying-on of hands". Well, a friend of mine was very ill and in a lot of pain, and I was sitting with him while his wife went out to do a bit of shopping. I thought, if only I could do something for him, and I remembered what you'd said in your sermon. So I got hold of his hands and prayed, "Lord, whatever is hurting my friend, please drive it out and give him peace"—and you know, the pain left him and didn't return.' His eyes filled with tears as he recalled the incident. 'You know, Mrs Cundiff, I've never told a soul about that. Folk would have laughed at me and said, silly old fool, but I know it was God who answered.'

I felt very humble, standing in the presence of that man

48

who had taken those words and acted on them. The following Sunday, as he read the lesson in a clear, strong voice, I thanked God for him, and for his own way of saying 'thank you' to God.

8

. . . TO COMFORT AND HELP

She was the most miserable, disagreeable person I think I have ever met. Her house, though old-fashioned, was clean and tidy. The coals burned brightly in a spotless grate. It was a pleasant and homely scene, except for the old lady herself, who was hunched miserably by the fire.

We sometimes make the mistake of thinking that old age turns people into saints—it doesn't! Most people become, when they are old, whatever they have been in earlier years. The cheerful, outgoing person will be the same in old age as in youth; the moaners and the groaners will be just the same as the years go by. A hard fact, but true! And this one was the prize moaner of all time. I had been warned by others who had visited her. 'You'll not get anywhere,' they said. Clergy, social workers, doctors, neighbours, all had tried, but to no avail. She moaned and complained about everybody, from 'the guvverment' to those who visited her, her neighbours—she didn't have a good word for anyone.

Trying to draw her out, I asked her about her early life—and then I got it!

She had married over sixty years ago, but her husband had left her after a very short time. Those who knew them in those days told me he was a saint. I could well believe them. After a divorce, he had married again, and from all accounts had lived a very happy life until his death some time ago. It was evident from what Mrs Wilde said that there had been no love lost between them. Rather, her anger was because she'd 'bin robbed', and she poured out with venom what she thought of ''er wot stole my 'usband.' I listened patiently. Maybe, I thought, if she gets it out of her system she will feel a bit better.

I was mistaken. Each time I visited her, I had the same story, and I began to realize that the recounting of it gave her a great deal of rather perverse pleasure. On one visit, as she again, and at length, told me her story, she suddenly stopped, looked at me and said, 'There's only one word for a woman like that, as pinches other folks' 'usbands, and it's a very naughty word, but . . .'

She faltered, stopped, and stared at me intently. Fascinated, I wondered what was coming next.

Her eyes were bright and angry, rather like a bird's. 'I can see you are a woman of the world, so I'm going to say that word, though it's a very naughty word.'

The back of my neck began to go hot. Sitting bolt upright, her mouth set in a firm line, Mrs Wilde delivered herself of the shocking word. 'She . . . she's a *faggot*.'

I felt a giggle beginning and hastily turned it into a cough. Mrs Wilde looked triumphant. 'There! I've said it, and I'm not sorry, even though it is a naughty word.'

Poor old soul, I thought, as I left. All those years, nursing hatred, resentment, anger. What has it done but turn her into a sour, warped old woman? What a waste!

It was coming up to Christmas. I kept thinking of my little old lady. Perhaps if we went to sing her some carols we might bring a little joy into her home.

'Oh, I don't think I could stand that, folk in my house,' she moaned, when I suggested it. 'How do I know they won't pinch anything?' Gently, I explained that we would all be from the church, and that anyway she would be able to watch us. I was tempted to offer to frisk everyone before they came in! She said she'd think about it.

The vicar called and raised the matter again. He came back shaking his head. 'She says no.' He laughed. 'She must have heard us sing before, because when I asked if a group could come and sing carols she said, "Oh, no, I just couldn't a-bear it!" '

I took her a parcel of things we hoped might give her pleasure. She merely grunted and said, 'I don't like any of that, you'd best take it back.'

What do you do with someone like that? Perhaps all we can do is go on trying, go on praying, and go on seeing her as someone God loves and wants the best for. And try by his grace to show her we love her too.

For some time part of my job was helping the chaplain at the large general hospital in York. I was 'doing a ward' one afternoon, and felt I was doing quite well. The patients seemed pleased to see me, and responded to my cheery 'And how are you?' with a catalogue of their operations or illnesses, told me about their families and seemed genuinely pleased that 'the church' had called.

I consulted my list. Nearly done, I thought, then a cup of tea and home. I was rather pleased with myself. Thirty visits—not bad for an afternoon.

'And how are you?' I asked the man in the end bed. He looked half asleep, lying on his side, with the sheets drawn up to his face. His expression was weary, drawn and haggard, as if with more than just physical pain. I suddenly felt unsure of myself, half wishing I hadn't approached him.

'How am I?' he grumbled. 'I'm here to die. I've got no legs, there's nothing the doctors can do, my wife has left me, no one comes to see me, and you ask me how I am! *You* tell me how I am.'

I drew up a chair and sat beside his bed.

'I suppose you're going to talk about God. Well, I don't want to know. What sort of a God would do this to a man?'

Anger had brought some colour to his face. I took his hand and introduced myself.

'I don't know the answer,' I said. 'I'm not God. But I really believe he can help you if you'll give him a chance.'

He began to tell me about his life. He'd been a keen cyclist and had worked as a gardener until this illness had gradually robbed him of his strength, and of everything he held dear. Now he would lie here until he died.

He nodded towards his locker. 'There's some photos there, have a look.'

I got them out, tattered snaps of a smiling couple with a tandem, of country scenes, of a young man in army uniform, or standing in a garden, with sleeves rolled up, eyes screwed up against the sun, holding a garden fork. Of the same young man on the bowling green, watched by other young men.

'That's what it was like before this,' he said.

I didn't talk much on that visit. There seemed nothing much to say. As I stood up to leave I asked if I could say a prayer with him.

'If you like,' he said, indifferently.

Taking his hands in mine, I prayed for God's love to fill him, for strength, for joy. I added a silent prayer that I might be able in some way to help.

'Are you coming again?' he asked.

'I'm here every week. Shall I come and see you?'

'If you like,' he said.

I walked out of the hospital feeling a lot less confident. Thoughtfully I crossed the car park, got into my car and started the engine. I headed out past the hospital, through the streets bustling with people going home from work, housewives doing last-minute shopping, children laughing and playing; and I thought of Jack in his hospital bed, with his demand: 'You tell me how I am.'

A few weeks later, on a lovely day in late May, I drove again to the hospital, past gardens which were a riot of colour, with blossom hanging heavy on the trees, pink, white and red. The ward, too, was full of flowers, their scent mingling with the hospital smell. Even in here the air was warm, the sunshine bright, filling the ward with cheerfulness.

Jack was lying hunched up as usual.

'Lovely day,' I said brightly.

' 'Tis for them that can enjoy it,' he replied.

I immediately felt sorry I had said that. After all, I was free to enjoy the summer. It was unlikely that Jack would see it through.

I sat down by his bed. He looked at me apologetically. 'Sorry I was a misery, but I'd love to be out there, like I used to be, gardening, being on the bowling green, seeing the kids and the dogs . . .'

I tried to cheer him up. 'Well, the flowers and plants in here are lovely.'

'Hmm.' He sniffed. 'They don't have any idea how to look after them. They either drown 'em or let 'em die for lack of water. Plants and flowers want to be outdoors, like folk, not stuck in here.'

I had an idea.

'I won't be a minute, Jack.' I went and found the sister. 'Sister, would it be possible for Jack to go out, across to the park?'

She looked doubtful, then said, 'I suppose he could, in a wheelchair, if someone took him.'

'Could I?'

She smiled. 'Yes, if you think you could manage him.'

I dashed back into the ward. 'You are going out, Jack. We're going to the park.'

The nurses wrapped him up in blankets, settled him in the wheelchair and took us to the lift. So far, so good. We went down in the lift. I pushed him along the road, waited at the kerb, then started to cross.

'Careful,' he muttered.

'Sorry,' I apologized, remembering I'd been no dab hand with a pram when the children were little, always bumping into something. I was scared crossing the road with Jack. We seemed very vulnerable.

Inside the park we walked around for a while, then found a seat by the bowling green, where I sat with Jack's chair beside me. People came up and talked to us, children scampered by, and several dogs, tails wagging, came up to be patted. Jack sat drinking it all in. When I saw he was getting tired, I took him back to the ward. I felt exhausted.

'It's been lovely,' Jack said contentedly as he was settled back in bed.

'We'll do it again,' I promised.

We managed a couple more trips to the park that summer. I saw the world through Jack's eyes, all the things I took normally for granted—a cat stretching on a wall, a child playing with a dog, the bowls players intent on their game, women chattering as they pushed their prams. Everything was alive, people going places, doing things, making plans— things we hardly notice until we aren't part of them . . . like Jack.

Now, whenever I pass the park and see the flowers and the activity, I think of Jack, and all the other Jacks, who will never again be able to share in the ordinary, everyday things of life. Then I think of Jack not as he was but as he is, enjoying the new life, the life that Jesus called abundant. Jack the gardener.

I'm sure Jack is enjoying a garden and he won't be in a wheelchair, he won't be restricted or in pain. Jack is free . . . and so one day will all of us be.

It is a special privilege to be able to minister to the ill and the dying, to speak of Christ to those who are nearing the end of their earthly life. The relationship a minister develops with a dying person can be a specially deep one, and it was

55

an encounter of this kind, soon after I resumed parish work, that helped to confirm me in my belief that God was calling me to a ministry in the Church.

I'd had a message that a man in the village was dying and wanted to see a minister. Since I was 'standing in' for the vicar, it was over to me. I had no idea what I was going to be confronted with. All I knew was that here was someone who wanted help.

I could see as I entered the room that he was desperately ill. His bed was in the corner of the living room. It was a cheerful room, comfortable, full of family photographs, but all I saw was that man in the bed, his eyes bright in his sunken face. Before I could even speak he spoke to me: 'I want to know how I can find God.'

Eric was very ill indeed, in fact dying from cancer. A much loved husband and father, popular at work and with friends, he hadn't had a care in the world until he became ill. Gradually as he became worse he had realized he was dying and began to ask questions about the Christian faith, but without satisfaction. He told me, 'I have so many visitors, people come to see me, they are so good, but no one will talk to me about the things I want to talk about.'

It was just the first of many visits. Strange though it may sound, I always found them enjoyable. We talked about many things, mostly about Jesus Christ and his promises. Eric eagerly listened and discussed. He loved me to read to him from the Bible, but he was still unhappy.

One day he explained his problem. 'I'm a fraud, you know. When I was fit and healthy I didn't go to church or think about God. Now I've nothing to offer God, it's not right to come to him with just a fag end of a life.'

Gently I explained that it was never too late to come. If Jesus could accept a thief on a cross, then no one could say it was too late. 'God loves you, and wants you just as you are.'

Eric thought about this a lot and then as I held his hand one afternoon he committed himself to Jesus Christ.

As he deteriorated physically he grew spiritually. He was a radiant Christian. He used to listen for me coming down the side of the house and always had a smile for me, even when in considerable pain. He always asked, 'What time is it? What sort of a day is it?' I usually went around the same time, and my reply was nearly always, 'It's three o'clock, and it's a lovely day.'

A neighbouring vicar came in to bring Communion, and so we met around Eric's bedside, his wife, Kath, the vicar, the district nurse, Judith, who was a Christian from our own congregation, and myself. That living room was indeed full of life. It was not only Eric who was blessed, but all of us.

Each time I left him I'd say 'see you on —day', and he'd smile and reply, 'Yes, and if I'm not here you know where I'll be.'

The week before he died I found him in a lot of pain and very weak, but as he opened his eyes he smiled and said, 'I'm so looking forward to meeting my Saviour.'

The sun shone on the day of his funeral. As I walked up through the country churchyard to the grave I looked at the coffin and thought of Eric, more alive now than he'd ever been. 'It's three o'clock, Eric, and it's a lovely day.'

He had asked that we buy some Christian literature for putting in the church. 'I'd like to think it would help someone else to know about Jesus,' he'd said.

I learned a lot from Eric. He was very special to me, perhaps because he was the first person I'd ministered to in this deep way since my return to parish work.

With Eric I discovered that the last lap in the journey of life can be a most marvellous experience. It was my privilege to share part of that journey with him, and we enjoyed it together. Of course there were times of doubt, of sadness, of apprehension, but it was a joyful time. We laughed, we had fun together, and learnt together that he was not going blindly to a dead end but to a glorious future, a sure and certain hope. The joy was in sharing frankly the fact of his dying, facing up to it squarely, making plans for it—even to choosing hymns and readings for the funeral. And even this was a triumphant occasion, because it was an affirmation of the truth of Easter, discovered through personal suffering and through personal faith in Christ.

Eric died in his own home, surrounded by those who loved him, in the little house across from the churchyard where he was laid. He died knowing he was loved not only by his family and friends but by the One who received him into his loving and safe keeping for all eternity. Death, when it came, was no enemy but a friend.

But what of those funerals, known to every minister, when there is apparently no Christian faith? When whichever minister is on 'cemetery duty' finds himself or herself officiating at the burial of a complete stranger? When the mourners have not been near a church service for years, if ever?

Now that I am a deaconess, I often conduct funerals, and I know how bleak they can be when there is no background of love and faith.

The undertaker rang me late one evening. 'Mrs Cundiff, can you do me a funeral?'

I got out my diary. 'When?'

'Two o'clock . . . tomorrow . . .'

'Why the rush?' I asked, surprised. Usually we have several days' notice, which gives us time to visit the family and get to know them.

'They've got a holiday booked—Majorca.'

'Oh, well,' I grumbled. 'Of course, I'll do it, but I do like more notice.'

I arrived at the cemetery in good time, in fact with three-quarters of an hour to spare. The chapel was full of people, and there was a coffin ready and waiting. I went to find the undertaker. He was in 'the hut'.

'Whose funeral is that, then?'

'Yours,' he announced.

'But mine isn't until two.'

'Ay, but I told you, they're going on their holidays. They're on the minutes.'

Right, I thought. Two o'clock you said, and two o'clock it is. I settled down to wait.

At two o'clock precisely, I began. I used every psalm, all the prayers, and I preached a long sermon—long, even for me!—ignoring the uneasy shuffling which grew more obvious as the service progressed. I led the procession out of the chapel and up the path, taking it slowly, in spite of the rain. I was getting very wet—but so were they, I thought gleefully. The fur coats of the mourners were beginning to look like the ginger tom up the road on a wet night.

I looked into the grave at the coffin. *Ernest Jones, aged 86.* 'I never knew you, Dad,' I thought, 'but I won't let them rush you.'

The family was polite. 'Thank you for a lovely service,' they said, as they made off down the path. The undertaker looked at me and grinned. He didn't say anything; he knew by my contented smile that I had made my point.

They had all gone now. I took one more look at the grave. How sad! They couldn't give Dad a bit of time even at his funeral.

Time. We don't have to be clever, articulate or have any training to be able to give others that precious gift of time.

It is what everybody needs, and we are all too busy, too involved, too concerned with ourselves.

Time. Time I went home. Time. All the time in the world, I thought. I peeled off my wet cassock and turned the car for home.

9

AND SO TO SCHOOL

'Mrs Cundiff, is it *all right* for an angel to wear wellies?' She looks so anxious, this little angel in her white dress with tinselled wings—and her jeans tucked into her wellington boots.

It is the day of the school nativity play and carol service, rain-sodden and bitterly cold, so the headmaster has insisted that the children be warmly clad, regardless of the part they are playing. We mustn't risk colds and flu, especially at Christmas-time. But when you are eight and you are an angel, it does matter whether wellies are all right or not! I give her a quick cuddle.

'Now there's nothing in the Bible that says angels can't wear wellies, and I'm sure if they needed them they would have them.' She smiles, adjusts her tinsel and runs back to join the rest of the angelic throng.

So the eternal story is told once again by the youngsters, not just playing the parts, but being part of the events. Mary and Joseph, serious and proud, the shepherds in their dressing-gowns and tea-towel head-dresses (with wellies), the kings looking so regal, in spite of treading on each other's cloaks, as they make their dramatic entrance. Herod being chided by Mrs Herod ('Try to be nice to our visitors, dear'), and his villainous aside after addressing the travellers: '. . . and when you have found the child, come and tell me that I may worship . . . (*no chance!*)' The readers with heads held high, proclaiming in their delightful broad Yorkshire

62

accent the Gospel account of the coming into the world of Jesus Christ.

It is a marvellous thrill for me to be part of this, to share with these children in their celebrations throughout the year, and especially at Christmas-time. The vicar and I take the Friday morning assemblies and it is our delight to visit the school each week, to be welcomed by the children, to receive their confidences, to hear of the doings of families and friends, to visit the pets ('Will you pray for our hamster, please, Mrs Cundiff?'), inspect the schoolwork, admire new shoes.

With children you never quite know what will come next. At the end of one assembly a small girl eagerly waved her hand in the air.

'Yes?' I smiled encouragingly.

'Please, Mrs Cundiff, would you like to have a baby?' All faces turned in my direction; I mumbled a bit, trying to play for time. How was I to explain that, much though I liked children, with two teenagers of my own I certainly had no desire to begin again?

'. . . because my guinea pig is having babies, and you can have one if you like.' Phew! Panic over.

Telling them one day about the birth of Jesus, I explained that Mummy is the first person in the family who will know that a baby is on the way.

'And what,' I asked, 'is the first question that Mummy will ask herself?'

Too late, I saw the older children's impish grins and realized I'd let myself right in for it! I picked on the most innocent-looking little girl.

'Will it be a baby boy or baby girl?' Thank goodness! At some schools I would have got a very different answer. Fortunately for me our village school still retains a charmingly unsophisticated attitude to life.

The large comprehensive school in Hull is quite a different

63

matter. Into this enormous complex a group of us from the diocese went to 'show the flag'. Our brief was to talk to the pupils about our work as ministers, to share our faith, and to put ourselves in the 'hot seat' and answer any questions they cared to throw at us. Ralph, a priest, and myself had taken on, or been taken on by, a noisy fifth form. Together we weathered the questions which came thick and fast. It was rather like a game of pingpong, hitting the ball back and forth, scoring or conceding points. We began to relax, the youngsters as well as ourselves. They were obviously enjoying themselves. Then came the inevitable question.

'Sir . . . Do you believe in sex, sir?' The questioner was a lively looking lad sitting at the back.

My companion paled slightly, perhaps wondering what was coming next. But he answered gamely, 'Yes, I do.'

'Do you . . . do you have it, sir?'

He soon batted that one back. 'Well, since I am a married man with two children, that should be evident.'

'Sir, sir . . . Do you enjoy it, sir?' The whole class collapsed in laughter, the boys falling about, the girls giggling more nervously.

Ralph smiled too. 'Sure I do. God means us to enjoy it. It's part of his plan for us in marriage.'

They were quieter now, and we all enjoyed the rest of the session. As we prepared to leave, the same boy asked, 'Are you coming again?'

'If you'd like us to, we will,' we promised.

'Great!' came the reply.

Later, over tea in the headmaster's study, we told him how much we had enjoyed our visit.

'Rough lot you had,' he said. 'I sometimes wonder what will become of them.' We told him of that afternoon's episode, and he turned white with anger.

'Tell me which one it was, and I'll deal with him. I must apologize . . .'

We stopped him. 'No, we aren't annoyed, it was a very sensible question. Yes, of course they were trying us out, but it is important they should know we are normal people.'

We did go back, quite a number of times. They were a sceptical lot. 'If God walked through that door I would believe in him,' was their frequent comment.

I had a surprise for them! A friend of mine, a vicar, was playing the part of God in the York Mystery Plays. I asked him to come to the school with me.

We walked into the classroom together and he sat beside me. I addressed the class. 'You often tell me that if I would show you God you would believe he exists. Right?' They agreed that this was their problem.

'Then,' I said, 'I'd like you to meet God!' It was an excellent opportunity for my friend to tell them, not only about the part he was playing, but why, and about his own faith, and I sensed them warming to him. I would like to feel he made them think. Certainly it took the wind out of their sails!

In another class we met Rob, a young Christian. He was pleased to see us, and did his best to back us up, in spite of being howled down by the rest of the class. He stood up bravely and told us the difference Christ had made to him.

'Don't listen to him, miss, he's a poof!'

Rob wasn't going to be put down that easily. He drew out of his pocket a battered New Testament to read us something that had impressed him.

Another lad jumped to his feet and pointed an accusing finger. 'Call yourself a Christian? Look at the mess you've made of your Bible. We all got one at the same time, and look at mine.' He fished around for a while in his sports bag, then triumphantly held up a New Testament in mint condition.

With difficulty, I pointed out that Rob's was in such a

state because he used it! After the session, Rob came up to me, looking dejected. 'Sorry I wasn't much help, miss. I do try, but it's a bit hard . . .'

A bit hard! I did my best to encourage him and promised to pray for him. It was touching to experience his eagerness.

'You see, miss, I'm the only one in our house that goes to church—but I don't care. Isn't being a Christian *smashing*!' I felt humbled as I turned to go home.

How much value can we put on work with children, on exercises such as ours? Is it worth the time and effort?

Whenever I ask myself that question I see in my mind a figure out of my past, a small, ginger-haired boy with a freckled face, wearing the shortest of shorts. Peter was one of my cub scouts. He was always the first to turn up for church parade, to answer the Bible questions. He was the one who always listened eagerly. His parents never went to church, but he came regularly, joined the choir and became a server. I can visualize him now, walking alongside me through the woods where the pack had been playing games.

'Akela, I know what I'm going to be when I grow up.'

'Do you, Peter?' My mind flipped through the usual list of small boys' ambitions. Engine driver? Farmer? Pilot?

'I'm going to be a priest.'

I looked down at the small figure in cub uniform trotting along beside me. 'I hope you will be, then, Peter.'

He smiled at me. 'I will be, Akela.'

Peter's intention never wavered. Often regarded as the 'odd one out', he went through school, university, theological college, a curacy. Peter is a vicar now. I'm sure he is a good one. He knew that 'one plus God is always a majority'. Just as Rob in Hull knows, as so many other young people have discovered.

It saddens me when the Church fails to take the opportunities that young people provide. Yes, I know it's hard work, it's so often disappointing, it's costly in time, in effort and in resources. But if the Church doesn't do it, who will? Home? School? Can we be sure?

I look at the delightful youngsters in Friday morning assemblies in the village school, at the difficult teenagers in the city comprehensive, at the bored faces of so many young people who see no sense in the world around them, and I see myself at their age.

I wonder where I would have been if my first vicar had not cared about me, if unknown Christians had not cared enough to run Youth for Christ rallies, if church leaders had not been willing to give me their time.

What then?

10

CHANGES IN THE AIR

It was just an ordinary day in early summer. A pleasant day, a day for getting up to date with the housework, for catching up on letters, for sorting out odds and ends. I decided to tackle the ironing. Normally I like to use ironing time for thinking out sermons. There is something about the rhythmic, automatic swinging to and fro of the iron that makes an ideal background to serious thinking.

This time I decided to switch on the radio instead, listening with half an ear while gradually the stack of ironing became a neat, well-ordered pile of 'ready-for-wear'. My husband's and son's shirts, conventional 'Marks and Sparks' button-throughs, along with tee-shirts emblazoned with vivid pictures and slogans. The sports gear of a son and daughter, dresses, sheets, hankies—all the usual assortment of a family wash.

Cheerfully going up and down with the iron, I was drifting into a happy mood, thinking about what to have for tea, of the meeting I was to take in the evening, of plans for next week, when I became aware of a discussion on the radio. It was between women who had reached the magic age of forty, and what a prospect it was! Your hair falls out, your figure goes to pot, your children don't want to know you, your husband is always kept late at the office!

But my life isn't a bit like that, I thought, and I'm past forty. The more I thought about it, the more I realized how good life had been since I had become forty—the return to parish life, the fun, the excitement, the sheer bliss of being where I believed God wanted me to be, with the bonus of enjoying it. All right, so I wasn't a slender blonde beauty, but then I never had been—more a comfortable, fair-to-mousey, average sort of woman. We were a united, happy family, and life was getting better by the day.

At last I could stand it no longer. I turned off the radio, unplugged the iron, and got out the typewriter. Staring at the blank paper in front of me, I typed in my best two-finger manner, LIFE BEGAN AT FORTY. The memories came flooding back as I thought over the last few years. Without worrying about punctuation, paragraphs or full stops I typed on, pausing only to make the tea. I finished up several hours later with a pile of typescript.

Now what? It had served its purpose, I had got it out of my hair, but it did seem a shame not to send it somewhere. Why not to the programme which had sparked it all off? So off it went to 'Woman's Hour', and that was the last I expected to hear of it.

A couple of days later came the letter from the BBC. Yes, they liked my article (so that was what it was!). They would like to interview me for radio. What excitement! I had visions of a large BBC van with 'Outside Broadcasts' in shining letters making its way to our house. The neighbours would be filled with admiration. I was already basking in the glory of it.

A Morris 1000 drew up, and a friendly middle-aged lady with a tape-recorder introduced herself. Not quite what I had expected—but still!

We sat in the lounge and chatted. I'd forgotten it was an interview; it was just like being with an old friend. After tea she said, 'We'll let you know when it will be broadcast.' The excitement mounted in our house until the letter arrived, with a cheque and the date of the broadcast.

The date . . . it rang a bell somehow. I looked in my

diary. Oh, no! It was the day of the church outing to Bridlington. I wouldn't even hear the broadcast.

However, armed with a transistor set, we sat on the sands, the children were shushed, and suddenly there it was. Was that really me? Did I really sound like that? What would people say? All of a sudden I wished I hadn't bothered. I felt dreadfully conspicuous and rather embarrassed. But then, I thought, people soon forget. It's been fun, an interesting experience, something I can tell my grandchildren when I'm an old lady, about 'the time I was on the wireless'.

What I didn't realize then was that it was the start of a whole new chapter in my life. That soon I was to be on the other side of a microphone, as an interviewer, that I'd be meeting people I'd only read about or seen from afar; that from now on my 'congregation' was to be increased by 'listeners', and in two or three years' time by 'viewers'. But that was in the future.

On reflection, after the spate of letters and phone calls had died down and a little time had passed, I thought back on that broadcast. What had it all been about? I was embarrassed that I'd talked so much about myself—but perhaps what I'd been trying to say had come over, that life at any age can be thrilling and new if you allow God to take control.

It made me aware, for the first time, that I hadn't given anything up for God. I'd just opened myself up to him, and he had overwhelmed me with gifts. Gifts of opportunities, of friends, of new experiences. Gifts that have been bathed in tears—of joy and sorrow, of delight and sadness. The indescribable thrill and pleasure of baptizing babies. The privilege of sharing the grief of bereaved families when conducting the funerals of loved ones. The gift of being allowed to minister in God's name to so many, of being accepted as a minister and as a friend, of sharing at the very heart of people's lives.

71

Every day is, in one sense, 'just another day'. We think we know what it will bring, where it will lead, what we will do. I have found out that life is full of surprises, and that there is only one way to approach any day. As each new day comes, I open my eyes, stretch my body, and my heart sings, 'This is the day that the Lord has made. I will rejoice and be glad in it.'

And that is the story of my life!

11

INTO ORDERS

'No. Definitely no!'

I had my limits, and I'd reached them. My life had been turned upside-down by God, and as soon as it seemed I'd got a breathing space, something else had come up which demanded an answer. I'd been, in my opinion, very adventurous, very obliging, but there were limits! Not that I was complaining; life was very rewarding, very enjoyable, and I could see that it had all been for the best, but . . . I dug in my heels. 'No, I'm just not cut out for that.'

'That' was a deaconess, and God was gently but firmly steering me towards becoming one.

I tried bargaining. 'Look what a lot I do already. It's not really fair to ask for anything more.'

I tried the reasonable approach. 'I'm a married woman with a family. What would they say?'

I tried to dodge the issue. 'They'd be sure to turn me down anyway.'

It was no use. I felt as if there was a gun in my back, forcing me forwards, and digging my heels in was becoming very painful.

I hadn't realized the pain was obvious until one morning at our staff meeting (rather an exaggerated name for the regular weekly meeting between the vicar and myself), as I was leaving, James said hesitantly, 'Are you all right, Margaret? You seem to have had something bothering you lately. I can't put my finger on it, but I thought you looked even close to tears once or twice, and it's not like you. What is it?'

I turned away and muttered into my anorak, 'What would you say if my position was different?'

'Come on,' he urged. 'Sit down. What's all this?'

I blurted out how I felt that God was calling me to be a deaconess, but it wasn't sensible, or practical, or possible; and I knew for sure James would agree with me.

He didn't bat an eyelid. 'I've been wondering for ages why you didn't do something about that.' That took the wind out of my sails.

'What does Peter say?' he asked. Peter had not been told. As I had not intended to do anything about the call, I had not discussed it with anyone. Now I would have to say something.

'Peter,' I began, as we were sitting watching television that evening, 'What would you say if I told you I felt God was calling me to be a deaconess?'

'I'd say, "Do you really believe this is what God wants for you?" '

I thought hard. Yes or no? The time had come to commit myself. 'Yes, I believe that is what he wants.'

'Then,' said my husband, 'I want it too.'

So, excuses, reasons and objections overruled on the home front, I set about applying. My bishop willingly wrote a reference, as did James and my former college tutor. I duly set off for the selection centre in London.

In the heart of the London dockland, the Royal Foundation of St Katherine is a centre where members of two religious communities live and work together, the Community of the Resurrection and the Deaconess Order of St Andrew. They work together as did the medieval brothers and sisters of long ago, using the building for many different purposes, including selection conferences. I entered the house from the busy roar of the London traffic, after a frantic dash from home, where up to the last moment before leaving I'd been baking for the family, making sure everything was done before I abandoned them for a couple of days. At once I found myself in a different world: a quiet world, a welcoming world of prayer and meditation. 'Even if they turn me down, it will have been worth it to come here,' I thought.

There were nine other candidates, of all ages, some married and some single women, and we soon got to know each other and the selectors. The chapel, where we went to join with the community in their prayers, was a taste of heaven. It was easy in that place to be totally frank with one another, to share how we felt. As we gathered on the final evening in the comfortable lounge to talk together before going our separate ways, I was suddenly aware of the cross the head deaconess was wearing—the cross which is the badge of the order. As it reflected the light it seemed to come into focus, as if seen through a camera lens, growing larger until all I could see was that cross in front of me. Perhaps there is no other way of describing it than to say that it said 'Welcome'. Then I became aware again of my surroundings, of the other people around me and of one of the selectors saying, 'We will of course be writing to you within the next few days to let you know.'

I knew before the letter arrived. I'd known for sure that last night at St Katherine's. The Archbishop of York wrote to me in his warm, personal style:

Dear Margaret, I am writing to confirm that I have now had a letter to say that you have been recommended for the Order of Deaconess—and more than that, warmly recommended! I need hardly say that I am delighted at the news and wish you every blessing in all that lies ahead. Yours, as ever, Stuart.

After the excitement had subsided, it was time to get

down to practicalities—the right gear! Where else but those well-known 'makers of robes for the clergy, and choir and clerical outfitters of repute'? I took a day trip to London and marched in, but I had not got far before a large gentleman blocked my way.

'Can I help you, madam?' He seemed not to approve of 'madam'!

'I want a cassock.'

He looked at me suspiciously. 'Deaconess? Come this way.' He led me into a room full of half-made robes and left me. I peeped at some of the labels. Obviously quite a few new bishops had been here before me.

The man returned, bearing a tape-measure. 'I shall have to measure you, madam.' I thought he still looked at me rather coldly. 'I shall have to ask you to take off your coat.'

I was wildly tempted to say, 'I'll take the lot off if you like,' but decided the gentleman was not in the mood for jokes. Solemnly he noted down the measurements. 'Some deaconesses are very fussy,' he informed me. 'Some are very hard to please.' I was duly warned! 'We will let you know when to come for a fitting.'

Some time later I was summoned for the fitting. I stood still obediently while the gentleman moved round me murmuring instructions through a mouthful of pins. He then decided he had to leave me for a few minutes. I scrutinized myself in the mirror. I did look rather strange. I put my hands into the pockets. Nice and full; I'd be able to carry everything around in those, they were big enough for the weekend joint. There seemed to be a slit next to the pocket. This puzzled me, but I didn't like to complain, especially after the warning about 'fussy deaconesses'.

When the gentleman returned I duly praised the work-manship. He seemed pleased, and almost smiled.

'But I think something has been overlooked,' I added meekly. 'There is a slit just by the pocket.'

He looked at me pityingly. Obviously I was very new. 'That is not an error, madam,' he informed me. 'That is so you can get your hand into your trouser-pocket.'

The ordination was to take place at York Minster at Michaelmas. Seven priests, seven deacons and me. The three days before the ordination were spent in retreat at Bishopsthorpe. It was a strange feeling saying goodbye to the family, knowing that the next time I would see them would be in the Minster on Sunday. The Archbishop was concerned for my husband. 'Is it all right if I have your wife for three days?' he asked.

Peter grinned at him and replied, 'Certainly. If you can do any better with her in three days than I've done in the last seventeen years . . .'

The three days were glorious. The autumn sunshine, the quietness of Bishopsthorpe, the helpfulness of the Bishop of Hull, who conducted the retreat, the charming hospitality and friendship of the Archbishop and his wife, and the company of my fellow-ordinands made it very special. I slept at the home of Mr and Mrs Kelly, the Archbishop's chauffeur and his wife. They made me very welcome, fussed over me with hot-water bottles and tea in bed; nothing was too much trouble.

I slept well on Saturday night and awoke to a bright blue sky, a fresh day. I knew myself to be surrounded by love and prayer and felt joy, confidence and a new assurance. We all met at breakfast, the new deacons fingering their dog-collars, looking very new, while those to be priested gave a few tips to the first-timers. We had come together as strangers; we set off for the Minster together as a family. It was a good day.

'Thank you, Lord,' I said, 'for insisting on your way.'

The Minster was filling up fast as we entered by the side door. There was an air of excitement, with a buzz of conversation, and the officials hurrying round to see that everything was in order. I caught a glimpse of my family, husband Peter, the children, Julian and Alison, and my parents, near the front. Friends and members of my congregation caught my eye and waved. I felt reassured, and very happy that so many had made the journey to be alongside me and share with me on this day.

There was a tap on my shoulder. 'All wired for sound?'

I turned to see one of my local radio friends. 'Okay for an interview straight afterwards?'

I nodded. 'Afterwards' seemed a world away. I suddenly felt desperately tired, and I remembered when I had felt like this before. It had been just prior to the births of my two children. Just at the point of the last push I had decided I was too exhausted and had pleaded, 'Can't it wait? Give me time!' But of course I had had to get on with the job, and I was going to have to get on with it today.

I walked down to where the other candidates were in various stages of robing. I practised walking up and down in my cassock. I was beginning to get the hang of it, but what if I tripped over and went flying? I stuffed my hands into the deep pockets, lost in thought until a voice bellowed behind me, 'Get your hands out of your pockets, Smithy!' It was a college friend of mine, now a deaconess herself, who had come up from London to be at my ordination.

'You don't improve any,' she said, and laughed. 'Do you remember how you used to keep your socks up with elastic bands?' It was good to see her, another loving expression of concern for me.

Then in procession we moved forward, the organ filling that huge, beautiful building with sound, the congregation joining in the hymns and praises. Later I stood before the Archbishop and bishops to affirm my belief and knelt for the 'laying on of hands'. I hadn't really expected that sudden rush to the head! Many, many hands laid upon me, a feeling

of being submerged in a sea of hands, going down under the pressure; then an experience of warmth, of power, of lightness. I returned to my seat with great thankfulness to God and to the Church which had accepted me.

At the end of the service I was reunited with my family, friends, and members of my church. But first came the interview for radio.

'. . . and do you feel any different?' the interviewer asked.

There was no doubt in my mind. 'Yes. I don't know how to describe it, but I am different.'

What had happened? Did the laying on of hands make any real difference, or was it my imagination? One of the letters of good wishes I had received from a parish priest put into words how I felt about that day.

I'm writing to wish you every joy and blessing on Sunday, and in your ministry as a deaconess. In a small sense it is a formality, isn't it? You have been doing the work of a deaconess for some years—but I pray that the grace of orders and the authority that goes with ordination will vastly increase your scope in the service of our Lord. Sorry if this all sounds so horribly pompous written down like that, but there will be an outpouring of God's grace and our prayers here at S—— will be holding you up.

Our church members had enjoyed the service terrifically. It had been a great experience for them to see 'our Margaret' well and truly 'done'. Michael expressed his pleasure in typical north-country fashion. 'It was a good do. The bit I liked best was when they got into the scrum and you disappeared. I thought to myself, any moment now someone will throw her out and run to touch with her!'

A year later there was again an ordination in York Minster. My friends the deacons were there, again to have hands laid on them; this time they were to be ordained priests in the Church of England, able to celebrate the Holy Communion, solemnize marriages, pronounce absolution and bless the congregation. I was not there with them, the reason being that I am a woman and they are men.

One of them rang me the day after the ordination. 'We thought of you and prayed for you. We said, "We are one short; Margaret should have been with us." '

Margaret thought so, too! Perhaps one day the Church will agree with us.

12

IN LOVE AND CHARITY

It had all started so pleasantly. James and I were in the vestry preparing for a midweek Communion service and chatting about various parish affairs. I reminded him about the Deanery Synod meeting to be held that evening.

'Oh, yes, that,' he said, and laughed. There was to be a debate on the proposals for the ordination of women, and I was to speak in favour. 'I don't know who is speaking against,' I said.

Without looking up, he replied, 'I am.'

I felt the anger surging. 'Hey, that's not on! We work together. I refuse to argue publicly with you. We have a good relationship even though we don't see eye to eye on this issue. It's just not on!'

James quietly went on with his robing. 'Don't you worry about that, Margaret,' he chuckled. 'I'll let you down gently.'

I stood there in my cassock, clutching a bottle of Communion wine in one hand and the chalice in the other. I wondered which to hit him with and decided the bottle was more expendable. Seething, I glared across at him and realized he had no idea he had said anything to offend or hurt me. I turned to take off my cassock. There was no way I could go into the church and take a Communion service with him, feeling as I did.

Then I thought of the congregation. What would they think if I walked out? I just could not do that. So together we entered the church, knelt at either side of the communion table, and began the service.

83

'Almighty God, unto whom all hearts are open, all desires known, and from whom no secrets are hid . . .'

'Lord,' I prayed, 'I am not in love or charity with James. I'm sorry, but please help me . . .'

I would like to say that love poured into my heart, but it didn't. 'Right,' I thought. 'Just you wait.'

And wait we did. We did not debate against each other that evening, but neither did we discuss the matter. Grimly I decided to wait my time.

The opportunity came through a telephone call from Yorkshire Television. The General Synod was to debate women's ordination that week, and they wanted to film me, as a typical woman minister, to show on the evening of the debate. I would then be in the studio to comment on the Synod's decision as it came through.

I asked James's permission and he gave it, though without enthusiasm. I realized that now I had my chance to bring out my feelings of frustration, my anger which had been steadily growing. I resolved to have my say, loud and clear, in front of a large audience. At last I would get my own back. 'Let me down gently' indeed!

The morning of decision day arrived. As I woke up and saw the sunshine I knew that anger and bitterness were no answer, but what could I do? I was all too conscious of my fiery nature, and I knew it spelt disaster. I rang a friend, a priest. Strangely, although we were good friends, I had no idea of his views on the ordination of women; we had never discussed the matter, and I didn't want to know now.

I explained to him how I felt. 'Will you pray with me?' I asked.

'Of course,' he agreed instantly. 'Why not in the context of a Communion service?' And so later that morning I drove out to meet him in his village parish. The church had a welcoming air, an atmosphere of peace and calm. Together we shared the Holy Communion, and as we exchanged 'the

85

peace' and he held my hands, I felt the anger and bitterness evaporate.

'I give you a word from the Lord,' he said. 'When you go into that studio tonight, remember this: "Surely the Lord is in this place, and I knew it not." '

I knew the Lord was in this place, this mellow old church with its prayer-filled walls, its very atmosphere a benediction. It was no problem here to feel at peace with God and man—but a television studio?

Later that day I walked through the entrance to the studios ('Surely the Lord is in this place'), into the green room to wait for the programme to begin ('Surely the Lord is in this place'), into make-up, and finally into the bright lights of the studio itself, with the interviewer beside me.

'The count is now being taken at the Synod,' he told me. 'We are having the result rushed through as soon as possible.'

The evening news programme began, then a piece of paper was put into my hand. The interviewer smiled gently at me. 'Sorry,' he said. 'I'm afraid the vote went against you. Are you all right?'

The commercial break was now on, and the cameras were being brought into position for our interview. The floor manager raised his hand for us to begin. 'Surely the Lord is in this place, and I knew it not . . .'; but I did know it. He was in this place. His presence filled it. I knew it right through to my innermost being.

The interview went out. I don't remember much about it. The telephone started ringing even before I reached home. There were congratulations on the calm way I had taken the news, the way I had dealt gracefully with the subject. But the remark I treasured most was from a friend who paid me a very back-handed compliment. 'Margaret, you were radiant on the television, you looked even beautiful!' Any radiance was none of my doing, the beauty was not mine. It was the reflection of the One who was indeed in that place that night.

Going into Yorkshire Television is now an everyday affair for me. In 1979 I was appointed Anglican Adviser to the company, the first woman Anglican Adviser to an ITV company. Each time I walk through the doors to meet those who have now become my friends and colleagues, I take with me that verse: 'Surely the Lord is in this place.' I know it. I prove it. And I go on in that sure knowledge.

Although life returned to normal after this, and James and I worked together very happily, there still remained a slight question-mark in my mind about our relationship. Neither of us mentioned the events that had gone before, but I always felt a pang of regret that we had not 'bottomed' the problem.

Then quite out of the blue one day, James said, 'I've been thinking about the Communion service; I'd like to do it slightly differently.'

My hackles rose at once. 'What's he going to stop me doing?' was my automatic reaction.

He went on, 'It doesn't seem quite right my receiving, then coming over to you. We are the ministers in this place. Why don't we kneel down together, and receive together?'

I happily accepted his suggestion, and the following Sunday morning we knelt together in front of the Table, we took the bread together, and James said, 'The body of our Lord Jesus Christ which was given for *us* . . .' Given for us! The last vestige of hurt had gone, had been dealt with in that moment of realization of what Christ had done for us both.

I tried to get up. I couldn't—James was kneeling on my cassock and, being a gentleman, was waiting for me to get up first! I hissed at him, 'Will you get off my cassock, please?' He grinned back, we stood up and together turned to face the congregation as they came up to the communion rail.

There were one or two puzzled looks from the congregation as they left the church. They were obviously aware that something had been different, but were not quite sure what it was. It was old Mrs Barnes who asked me, 'What were you and the vicar doing when you both got down on your knees? Had you lost something?'

I opened my mouth to try to explain but decided it was too complicated.

'Actually,' I said, 'we had just found it!'

I suppose there will still be a lot of heartache ahead as the debate goes on about the rôle of women in the ministry. People are going to be hurt on both sides, relationships will be affected in many ways. It's inevitable, really. It will only be as we see each other as brother and sister, as we love each other as we are, with all our fears and hang-ups, with all our vulnerability, and are able to say, 'Jesus died for *us*', that we will be able, by the grace of God, to cope and to accept, whatever is the outcome.

13

WHY CAN'T A WOMAN . . .?

I was having a cup of tea with the hospital chaplain after visiting some parishioners, when another priest, a stranger to me, approached us. I thought I detected a slight gleam of mischief in the chaplain's eye as he introduced us, then, excusing himself, disappeared with what seemed indecent haste. Perhaps he knew something that I didn't.

As we exchanged small talk the newcomer eyed me carefully from head to foot and back again, with an expression of the utmost disapproval. Then: 'I suppose you want to be a priestess like they all do,' he challenged, and waited for my reaction.

I went on drinking my tea. After what I thought was a suitable pause, I looked him straight in the eyes.

'If you mean do I want to dance in the moonlight at pagan rites, not at all. I believe I am called to a Christian ministry within the Church of England. I don't think the two have anything in common, do you?'

Snorting with indignation, he made off down the corridor, with an angry swirl of his cassock.

The chaplain returned a few minutes later, smiling quietly to himself when he saw I was alone. 'Did he have a go at you about women's ordination?'

I told him of our brief conversation, and he laughed. 'You are dreadful, Margaret. You knew what he meant.'

Of course I knew. It was by no means the first time I'd been confronted with that word—priestess. 'We will not tolerate priestesses in the Church', thundered an article in

the religious press. The word is an emotive one, conjuring up pictures of pagan sacrifice and nameless orgies, presided over by frenzied women ringleaders; everything contrary to the concept of the Christian minister. Its very use is calculated to arouse antagonism to admitting women to ordination. Besides, who ever speaks of a 'doctoress' or 'judgess'?

Opposition is not always so blatant. It can take more subtle forms. There is the 'we love you as you are' approach: 'You do such splendid work; you don't want to be like a man, do you?'

There was even the friend who suggested that wearing a cassock wasn't feminine! 'I wouldn't want you to look like a fella.'

My answer to that was, 'With my figure? Impossible!'

Over the years I have become quite adept at replying to those who attempt to bully or cajole me out of my belief that God has called me to serve him as a priest. I suppose I often use humour as a defence when they try to belittle what I believe is right for me. I am a fairly resilient character. But still I am often deeply hurt, and have to learn to accept the 'slings and arrows' as part of the cost of my calling.

How do I know I'm called to the priesthood? How does anyone know, except by a deep inner conviction that has nothing to do with status, or with function, but with 'being'? This is true for any calling, whether the recipient is male or female. I've heard all the arguments, for and against, many times, and in many guises. I can see, and deeply sympathize with, the very real difficulties that people face on both sides of the fence. I have close friends who are totally opposed to women's ordination; but it has made no difference to our friendship, as people, as fellow-Christians, as working colleagues. As one friend said, 'Never mind, we still love you.' And that is what matters.

I have often been regarded as militant—in fact one

newspaper described me as 'battling Margaret'. Yet I have never seen this issue of women's ordination as a banner-waving exercise or a shouting match. Rather, it is a matter of being true to my own belief, which includes the challenges and restrictions as they are. It saddens me that, simply because I am a woman, I cannot have my vocation tested by the Church. Yet I am quite sure that I must work within the constraints of the Church to which I belong. I accept its authority, while looking forward to the time when, as I believe, the Church will accept me as a person who has a vocation to the priesthood.

The General Synod's decision that women as well as men can be made deacons gave great hope to me, and to others in my position. It was not only the decision, that overwhelming show of hands—and as a member of Synod I was there when the vote was taken—but the new attitude. There was an obvious awareness of how women felt, and still feel; a new openness and desire to know and to do what is right, whatever it costs.

So what is the future for my ministry? I find my work as a deaconess very satisfying and rewarding. In accordance with Canon Law of the Church of England I can say Morning or Evening Prayer ('save for the Absolution') and distribute the Sacrament at Holy Communion. I can preach, baptize, take funerals, publish banns of marriage, and on the rare occasion when it is requested, conduct the service for the churching of women. On the other hand I cannot celebrate Holy Communion, hear confessions, absolve or bless, or perform marriage. I can, of course, carry out pastoral duties of many kinds. Since I took my first very uncertain steps into 'full-time service', things have altered beyond recognition. There is ample scope in so many different fields of service for women, and I rejoice in this latitude.

But it does not change my growing conviction, especially since I have been a deaconess, that I am called to be a priest within the Church of England. I go on day by day in the knowledge of that calling, believing that in God's time—not in man's, or woman's—it will come.

Meanwhile I have to accept the fact that for a woman working in the Church, whether as a lay worker or a deaconess, the fact that she cannot be ordained priest means that she is always an assistant, answerable to the vicar, who is the 'man in charge'. It means that whenever a vicar leaves, she has to face the prospect of a new 'boss'; and it is not always easy making a new relationship, particularly if she has spent a long time working with one man and has got used to a certain pattern of working.

Working with an Irish vicar for seven years was quite an experience for me. When James first came to the parish, not long after I had been licensed, he asked me, 'Do you think we will get on?'

I looked at him, this large Irishman, with his mop of dark hair and his lively smile. 'Yes,' I assured him. 'I think we will get on, but there is one problem; I think we are very alike, and we may fight.'

We did get on, very well. We were very alike, both very determined people. And we did fight, now and again! What saved us was a similar sense of humour. We found that we could laugh with each other, and this ability soon got rid of any real problem in working together. Working with James was an adventure, and great fun. We never knew what would happen next; as he said, we worked 'on the wink and nod principle'. We ad-libbed like mad, yet somehow knew each other well enough for it to look like organization. I knew, when the time came for him to leave us, that I would miss him. It would be like losing a brother. I could hardly imagine what it would be like to have someone else opposite me in church, someone else sharing the vestry, sharing the ministry. I felt very sad, and a little apprehensive.

Then David came, a Londoner, a quiet, gentle man.

From the very first I warmed to him, yet it was some time before I felt the ease I had had with James. I was not sure how he would respond to my high spirits, so I treated him with a certain degree of reserve. I wondered what he really made of me; whether indeed he even approved! I grew to like him more and more, yet there was still a slight reserve on my part.

Then it was decided that we would have a regular service of laying-on of hands with prayer for healing, at our evening Holy Communion service once a month. We had had several of these services before David came and I wondered how it would work out now. As the time came for the laying-on of hands I turned towards him, for we were to minister together. Before I could say or do anything he had knelt down, looked up at me and asked me to pray for him. At that moment any reserve I had disappeared. I knew David was accepting me as I was, as me, as a colleague and as a fellow-servant of Jesus Christ. To kneel and ask your assistant to pray for you, I reckon, takes real grace, and it left a very deep impression on me and on my attitude in the ministry.

Much has been said and written about the isolation and loneliness of many Christian ministers, who often feel that they are put on a pedestal by their congregations, are always expected to take charge, to know all the answers and cope with all the problems. This of course is true, but could not the problem be in some cases that the minister makes it that way? He or she finds it hard to ask anyone for help, to admit to a need; and so it becomes a vicious circle.

This is how it often is with me. I am a fiercely independent character. Even Peter my husband, tells me, 'The trouble with you is that you won't let people help you,' and I know that's true. There are times when I know I need help, but I go on stubbornly trying to cope on my own. Fortunately for me I have friends, including my bishop, who recognize the warning signs and take me in hand—and thank goodness they do! When I do try to push away those who want to help me, when I do find myself becoming proud of my own self-sufficiency, I see again a man who was big enough to ask me to pray for him, and I realize how much I need the prayers and support of others, and especially of those whom I work alongside in the ministry.

14

IT'S ME, O LORD

'Sorry you had to make such an early start this morning,' said my companion as she opened the car door and I hopped in beside her. It *had* been an early start coming in to meet her in York from my home, but we had a meeting in the north and had agreed to travel up together.

I settled myself down in the passenger seat and was just about nodding off to sleep, when my friend said, 'I don't know how you do it, fitting everything in, and saying your prayers.'

I gave some sort of lame reply and gazed out the window. My companion chattered on, mercifully changing the subject. She didn't realize her words had caught me on a very tender spot, for the truth was I hadn't said my prayers; in fact with all the rush, prayer had been the last thing on my mind.

Sometimes I think, 'If I hadn't the sort of job I have . . .' or 'If I was a different sort of person . . .' prayer would be so much easier. I would be able to turn to prayer and study so easily, it would not be the constant battle it is.

Yet I find in the struggle and in the failures—which are many—I am brought time and time again to rediscover the graciousness of God. There are times when prayer is hard, when my words and thoughts bounce back at me like tennis balls, when I open my Bible and it's words, words, words, as dry as the paper they are written on; but I do know whose fault it is—mine! Then it is as though God gives me a gentle dig in the ribs and says, 'Come on now, settle down, I want to talk to you,' and I relax into his presence.

There is built into us a feeling that God only speaks to us at certain times and in a certain way, and if we do not slot in then all is lost. I do try to make certain times in the day for prayers, for reading, but it's a variable time, and there are times, sadly, when it gets missed altogether; and yet there are many times in the day when I am so aware of the love of God surrounding me, when I'm driving along, or perhaps in a train, or even in a meeting, and I slip into prayer, as into the company of an old friend, and I bring with me people and events, problems and pleasures.

Some years ago a friend of mine was trying to describe an experience of prayer she had had, of being caught up into such an awareness of God that it was 'as if I could have reached out and touched him'. I found that at the time very difficult, if not impossible to imagine. I thought of it as very emotional, even sentimental. Prayer for me wasn't ever like that. Then one day I too came to this same experience. I could understand what St John was talking about when he said, 'I saw a door open in heaven . . .' I was drawn into that light and warmth and power. Since then it has happened quite a number of times. Sometimes in church, sometimes when walking or driving. I remember vividly one day on my way into York having to stop the car and just sit back and relax into it. It is then that, as the hymn puts it, I am 'lost in wonder, love and praise'. And it is when I hit the hard patches, and when I feel 'Is it worth the effort?' that I remember that God doesn't change. He is equally with me in the dark and dull as well as in the light and delight.

Prayer is a duty. I need to keep reminding myself that I have a duty to pray, and there can be no excuses. I asked my bishop about it one day when I was feeling a bit desperate, and he gave me some very good advice: 'Write your prayer-time into your diary; make an appointment with God,' he said. I try to do so, and it does work. But prayer is also an adventure, and sometimes I feel adventurous, and sometimes not! Yet it's when I am willing to launch out into prayer and I discover so much of God that I could kick myself for being so unwilling to be adventurous. For prayer is also a delight; there is nothing to compare with being totally taken up with God and in his presence.

There are so many books written on prayer, so much advice given, and yet the only way to discover what prayer is about is to practise it. So I shall go on no doubt making my mistakes, missing out, being downright disobedient—and I will be the loser, but I shall go on trying, and, I know, experiencing that God is listening and answering and surrounding me with his love.

And what of Bible reading? So often I sit down and open the book, and as I begin to read I'm already working out my introduction, points one, two and three, and conclusion. I jot down a few notes from my 'reference book' for the study group I'm leading tonight, and before I shut it I've flipped through the pages to find just the right story for the School Assembly on Friday—and while it's open I had better make a few scribbled 'thoughts' towards next Sunday's sermon.

What I've described is what often happens to me, and I suspect to other ministers. It has been described somewhere as 'the rape of the Word'. That sounds strong stuff, but it's true. So often I come to the Bible simply to take out what I want. It's a tool, a reference.

I find it hard to sit down with the Bible, open it and, for no other reason than that it is the Word of God, let it speak to me. I have the 'end product' always in the back, and often in the front of my mind: the need to produce something. The result is often a very good production and a dry me. It's something I fight with continually, a fight I often lose. Yet I find when I can sit down with the Bible just out of sheer love for it, out of the desire to hear God speaking

to me, then I am rewarded beyond measure. I am renewed by it, I am given fresh insight into what life is all about and, more importantly, what God is about.

Confessing all this to David one day I found out I was not alone with the problem, and we decided to put some time apart each week to get together and read through the set passages for that day; to share together, not as a theological exercise, or preparation for preaching, but as ministers to be taught by God's word. It's something I try to encourage other people to do, too, and I was very much touched when someone came up to me and said very shyly, 'I was reading the Bible the other day and you know, it was just like Jesus was there talking to me in our kitchen.' I reckon an encounter in the kitchen with Jesus is far more valuable than the most carefully prepared script from the pulpit— and I try to remember that as I sit down in my kitchen and open the book.

The act of worship, too, is something we ministers tend to take for granted.

I was in York one day for a couple of appointments and, passing a church, I saw a notice, 'Lunch Time Service'. I looked at my watch and saw it was just about 12.30. Decision time—home? lunch? or go in? I decided to go in and as the service had just begun was unnoticed.

So I slipped into the back row of the church and closed my eyes. What followed was one of the best half-hours in a long time. To be able to enjoy the music, relax during the worship and listen to someone else! I came out with a new outlook!

I suppose it was that experience that prompted me to 'drop in' whenever I am in the city, and especially if I am near the Minster. For me there is nothing like a sung Evensong in a minster or cathedral; it's a touch of heaven. I suppose for most ministers it's something they rarely can enjoy because of being 'one-man bands'. I'm fortunate in that for most services I'm sharing the leading and the preaching; but even so, to be part of a congregation—and especially one where I am not known—is a real pleasure.

Being part of the congregation means that I see the worship from quite a different angle. It makes me notice what a difference the minister's facial expression makes, the way he walks or sits. It focuses my view on the layout of the church, even the position of the flowers. Perhaps every minister should have to spend some time each year 'in the ranks' of a congregation; it may help him or her to overcome some drawbacks from the congregation's point of view. What we often forget is that our congregations have to look at us, whether they want to or not. I'd like to know what they think sometimes!

But of course, 'worship' isn't something we just do in church. I find going for a bike-ride or a walk often enables me to worship God in a very personal way. I'm on my own, I am surrounded by evidence of his creation—and that's often far more helpful than the most expensive stained glass.

I suppose I enjoy my worship most often when I am driving! This is the time when I enjoy my 'liberation' in worship. A friend once told me he used to pray in the car when he got to a certain point on his way home. One day he gave a lift to a hitch-hiker and, when they got near to his 'praying point', said, 'I hope you won't mind if I don't talk to you now, I always pray at this point.' His passenger looked rather scared, and then asked, 'You don't shut your eyes, do you?'

By the way, I don't either!

We need always to be alert to God's presence in the everyday of life.

On a morning when my head was full of all the things I had to do that day, when I felt every moment was 'spoken for', some words came like a shaft of golden sunlight into a grey day: 'Every minute of our lives is free time.' I was strap-hanging in the London Underground, during the rush hour, travelling to General Synod in Westminster, and I had already adopted the habit of other tube-travellers of reading a book while hanging on to a piece of metal to keep my balance, as more and more people pushed in at every station. Those words made all the difference to how I felt about the day ahead, the people I would see, the meetings I would attend, the work I had to do. It brought home to me afresh that I was living in free time. I couldn't buy time, demand it or earn it; it was absolutely free, a gift from God, and he wanted me to enjoy it—and so I would!

I wanted to shout to my fellow-passengers, those anxious-looking people squeezed in beside me, 'Hey, listen to this! Every minute of life is free time!'—but I didn't. Maybe they would not have appreciated my discovery!

So when people ask me, 'How do you manage to fit so much into your life?', my usual answer is, 'I don't know. All I do know is that God gives life a wonderful elasticity'—and it's true. I admit I am often busy, sometimes tired, occasionally frantic. And God knows just when to step into the situation when I come to the point of seemingly running downhill into chaos.

I don't think it was by accident that I was reading that particular book on that particular morning. I believe God knew the way to get through to me and say, 'Look at today this way.' I find God speaks to me in so many different ways: in people, in places, through books, even through a joke.

I once said to Cardinal Suenens in a radio interview, 'You are a very unusual person. You are a cardinal, and yet part of the charismatic renewal movement. How can you adapt your life to all the varied demands?'

He smiled at me and replied, 'When I was a young man I saw scribbled on a wall these words: "You cannot direct the wind, but you can adjust your sails." I just allow the Holy Spirit to take hold of me.'

I've often thought about that—'You cannot direct the wind, but you can adjust your sails'—and I try to adjust my sails so that his wind can take me in the right direction.

15

. . . AND THEN IT'S MONDAY AGAIN

Monday morning in our household is the same as for millions
of others, I suppose. The family gathering together their
bags and books, the cries of 'Where's my gym kit . . . clean
shirt . . . Who has moved my . . .?' Pop music from upstairs
competing with the radio downstairs. The crunching of
cornflakes, the click of the pop-up toaster, the shrill whistle
which tells me that the kettle is boiling. I'm beginning to
gather my wits, for during all my married life my day has
begun in bed with a mug of coffee being placed beside me
by my husband, who is a much better 'getter upper' than I.
(The only day the rôle is reversed is on Christmas morning,
when I take him a cup of coffee!) Then it's 'Where's my
dinner money? . . . see you tonight, mum,' and the youngsters rush for school and work.

Soon after, I wave goodbye to my husband as he sets out
on his day, and I begin to gather up the odds and ends left
behind from their flight. The washing machine swings into
action, and in no time at all order begins to return after the
chaos. With the washing pegged out, the rabbit having been
fed and chatted to and her nose well rubbed, I'm off!
Monday morning is the time when the vicar and I get
together to pray, to plan and to look back and forward.

We settle ourselves down at the vicarage with mugs of
coffee and go through the diary, reflect on the Sunday
services and the happenings in the parish. We look forward
to our week ahead, and we pray together. We pray for the
parish, for individuals and situations, and we pray for each

other and for our families. Both of us know how much we rely on our families, how much they have to put up with us as we try to cram so much into each day.

Then I'm off, for Monday is market-day, when our town is bright and noisy with stalls of all sorts. Whatever you want you can find here on Mondays. The loud shouts of the auctioneer who sells anything from chickens (alive and kicking) to cars (not so alive or kicking!). Fruit and vegetable stalls, flowers, china, clothes, second-hand articles, records, books and, one of my favourites, the 'sweetie man', chocolate and sweets cascading down, jelly babies, caramels, allsorts, boxes, packets, bags. His line in patter is an education—and I fall for it every time!

I don't get far before I meet people I know. I listen sympathetically to the tales of 'I've just come from the doctor's and he's given some more of those pink tablets, he took me off the green ones, they didn't do anything for me and . . .' Then there are the apologetic ones—'Sorry I didn't make it yesterday, I'll do my best next week . . .'—and the 'I'm glad I've seen you, I was going to give you a ring. We were wondering, could you come and speak to our Guild Meeting . . .?' I get out my diary and pencil in the date.

Often others we know stop and join with us until quite a small crowd gathers and some wit says, 'Is this a private meeting or can anyone join in?' or, 'What's this, a mother's meeting?' or, 'What are you collecting for, then?'

Finally with the shopping bag bulging I consult my list: 'meat, sugar, butter, birthday card, laces for shoes . . .' I begin to make my way back to my car which I've left at the vicarage. Oh yes, collect cleaning, pick up film. At last I make it back to the car and heave all my goods into the boot.

Then before I go home I get another key out of my handbag. It's the church key. I open the door and walk down to my stall and I sit down for a few minutes. It's quiet and peaceful, no sense of hurry. I relax. The building has a different 'feel' on a Monday morning from Sunday's. I think of the day before, seeing in my mind the children and young people, the older folk, the families. I can hear the hymns and the choruses. I look across at the other stall and thank God for those who have occupied it over the years, for David, who is the present incumbent, and my eyes catch those words over the organ facing me; 'Let everything that has breath praise the Lord.'

I think again of the week ahead, the demands, the deadlines to be met, interviews to be done, scripts to be written, people to see, sermons to be delivered. I think of all that I have to do, and sometimes I wonder, 'How on earth am I going to get through it?' And then I hear again those words which have been with me through my life, through all the ups and downs, the dull and the dramatic patches, the exciting and unnerving, in the sheer ecstasy and the utter boredom, in all the fun and in all the sadnesses; the words which are unchanging, and yet which never fail to thrill me: 'Fear not, for I have redeemed you. I have called you by name, you are mine.'

And it is as though all the lights come on at once, and I know everything is going to be just fine. I look at myself, and I laugh. I'm fifty—and I feel better than I did at fifteen!

I walk (and sometimes I have a little skip) down the aisle, I look down the church and I see that Table where yesterday I shared in the Holy Communion, where the Lord renewed and refreshed me, where by his grace I ministered and was ministered to, and I feel a great sense of anticipation. I wonder what will happen before I come again to that Table.

I remember the first time I came into this church and looked at it with the eyes of a stranger. Then it seemed dark, austere, even a little forbidding. Now I see it as a friend, a place of warm welcome. It's not beautiful, has little of material value compared with some churches, but it has a homeliness—the comfortableness of a trusted and loved

106

friend. Can a building be a friend? I believe it can; that's how I see it, anyway.

As I emerge into the busyness of Monday, of market day, of 'just another day', I often wonder to myself, 'Who am I really? What am I? Wife, mother, daughter—deaconess, broadcaster, TV adviser—friend, neighbour, colleague. Yes, but who is the real me? Does anyone really know?' I give a lot of thought to this question. I come up with many different answers, yet I know there is one sure and marvellous fact, which will not alter however I feel, whatever happens, and does not depend on what anybody else thinks; and it's this, the Word of the Lord to me:

'Fear not, for I have redeemed you. I have called you by name, you are mine.'

Called by name! God knows me, loves me, and has called me by name. I don't have to be anything but myself; I'm called to be me! So, does it matter what's round the corner? Does it matter what I'm labelled?

Down the road I go in my little red Polo, round the corner, through the market place, up over the bridge and I'm on my way home. It's a great life, and I wonder, what *is* round the next corner?

Also by Margaret Cundiff

FOLLOWING ON

In *Following On* we meet again the people of the parish, along with Margaret Cundiff's colleagues in broadcasting, her friends and her family. Once more we go behind the scenes in the life of a busy woman minister, as we accept her invitation to: 'Come and share with me the delights and the disasters, the fun and the failures. Come and meet the folk who share my life.'

I'D LIKE YOU TO MEET

Here are some of the people Deaconess Margaret Cundiff has encountered in her day-to-day life – in the parish, in broadcasting, in the supermarket or on the bus. Close friends or chance acquaintances, all have enriched her life and taught her more about God. That richness she now passes on through the pages of this book.